a space of my own

CAROLINE CLIFTON-MOGG

a space of my own

INSPIRATIONAL IDEAS FOR HOME OFFICES, CRAFT ROOMS AND STUDIES

RYLAND
PETERS
& SMALL

LONDON NEW YORK

Designer Paul Tilby
Editor Rebecca Woods
Picture research Emily Westlake
Head of production Patricia Harrington
Art director Leslie Harrington
Publishing director Alison Starling

Indexer Diana LeCore

Published in 2011 by
Ryland Peters & Small Ltd
20–21 Jockey's Fields
London WC1R 4BW
519 Broadway, 5th Floor
New York, NY 10012

www.rylandpeters.com

10 9 8 7 6 5 4 3 2 1

Text © Caroline Clifton-Mogg 2011
Design and commissioned photography ©
Ryland Peters & Small 2011

A CIP record for this book is available from
the British Library.

Library of Congress Cataloging-in-Publication Data

Clifton-Mogg, Caroline.
 A space of my own : inspirational ideas for
home offices, craftrooms, and studies /
Caroline Clifton-Mogg. -- 1st US [ed.].
    p. cm.
 Includes index.
 ISBN 978-1-84975-156-8
 1. Office decoration. 2. Home offices.
 I. Title. II. Title: Inspirational ideas for home
offices, craftrooms, and studies.
 NK2195.O4C62 2011
 747--dc23
                                    2011020153

ISBN: 978 1 84975 156 8

Printed in China

Contents

Simple to set up, as well as extremely functional, this room has been made into a dedicated, compact working space – with copious natural light, and one wall hung with enough shelves to hold all necessary books and essentials. The only other requirements are a large table, a comfortable, purpose-designed chair and a slim, good looking task light.

Creating An Inspirational Space

We all need a space we can call our own – and we always have; although today there are relatively few who can emulate in their own homes the grand designs of the architecturally distinguished studies and libraries of the past, nevertheless, the desire for a space of one's own apparently burns just as brightly. According to new figures, some 70 per cent of home renovation plans now include space for a home office or study of some kind.

The concept of a private and personal space for both men and women, is one that dates back to at least the 17th century, when the idea of a domestic, predominantly family life began to assume as much importance as the traditional more public life of the wider household. From around this time, houses began to be built with a number of small, rather discreet, rooms leading off the larger communal halls and reception rooms; it was in these cosier spaces that domestic life began to evolve. And it was in at least one

LEFT: A chair and desk in front of a picture window can be an inspiration. It is prudent, however, to install a blind that can easily be lowered when concentration is required.

BELOW LEFT: A large French window gives natural light and makes this room a peaceful place of retreat with an aura of calm and purpose.

OPPOSITE: An uncluttered area coupled with an abundance of natural light make this not only a perfectly arranged working space, but also a place of classic comfort, where constructive relaxation can be indulged!

of these small rooms – often then known as a closet or a cabinet – that a gentleman might have his collection of rarities: valuable printed books, small precious works of art and other curiosities, both from the natural world and man-made. Over time, this idea of a collector's cabinet evolved into the study, a peaceful place of retreat where not only could study and learning be pursued, but also where objects of interest and beauty were displayed, and such perceived masculine indulgences as smoking enjoyed. The female equivalent of this private space would have been the boudoir – part dressing room, part sitting room, decorated in accordingly female fashion, where the lady of the house might receive friends and follow such supposedly feminine pursuits as needlework or art.

We are not so different now – we still all like the idea of a retreat, and the very word 'study' still conjures up the idea of a small,

The correct lighting is of the utmost importance in any working space, large or small. Here, daylight is controlled by a wide-slatted venetian blind and augmented by a tall, angled desk light.

ABOVE LEFT AND RIGHT: A working space of your own can be as small and as contained as you like – as small indeed as simply a wall, alcove or corner that is large enough to hold a table and chair. Everything else is added luxury – although a good source of natural light is helpful, as is an electricity source and somewhere relatively close to hand to store work essentials. Over the centuries many a great work has been produced under such circumstances!

warm room decorated with some of its owner's most favourite possessions – always personal and usually reflecting his or her likes and pursuits. A space of your own is somewhere where you have around you the things that you both need and want, a haven that is both calming and creative at the same time, a shelter, and a place of peace; where you can be alone – even if there are others around – and where you should be able to write, work, read, or simply sit and think. Whatever your particular desire, the idea of a room devoted to one's personal and private passions remains immensely appealing.

Of course this desirable little haven may not be an entire room: it might be set up in a room with another purpose – a spare bedroom

2

The smallest of areas can become a private and personal work space. Look for a desk like this 'Covet' desk by Case that has integrated storage below and is deep and wide enough to keep the papers and books that you need about you.

OPPOSITE: A chair that will slide neatly beneath the desk surface between the built-in filing bins is a bonus in a small space. Natural light, boosted by an effective desk light, will allow you to work at any time of day.

perhaps, or a rarely used dining room; or it may be a carved-out space in a larger, busy room, or tucked away in a corner hitherto unused. The important thing is that it is known to all as very much your space, and it should feel private – not necessarily in a 'keep out' sort of way, more that it is not part of the general cut and thrust of the rest of home life, but somewhere specifically designed to cater to you and what you are doing – even if what you are mainly doing is arranging the rest of the family's lives.

In order to create a successful space of your own, it is important to first decide what

Try to create an area that is specifically designed to cater to you and your needs

exactly you will be using it for – apart from enjoying the general sense of well-being and peace as detailed above. Will it, for instance, be primarily geared for income-producing work, used to run a home business perhaps, or used as a place where work is done for an employer based elsewhere? Ever increasing

technological advances that bring instant communication between people, as well as more flexible working hours, mean that more people are able to work from home, and more companies would like them to do so.

Or perhaps you need a home office space from where you can organize your own life

and the lives of those around you, from organizing paperwork and finances, to family social life, and all the other often pleasurable, but always time-consuming, elements of domestic life.

For both of the above scenarios, the very use of the word 'office' might, at first, strike a small frisson of fear into the heart – a worry perhaps that it might all be just too grown-up and costly, as well as being ugly and utilitarian, to introduce office practice and equipment into your home. But an office is just a word and only as elaborate, or utilitarian, as you care to make it. It might involve almost no re-arrangement or expenditure at all, simply being you, a laptop and a phone at a table in the window. Or it could be a whole room

ABOVE LEFT AND RIGHT: A home office or work space that functions well can be composed of many different elements, both those designed for purpose and those that were not. Both these spaces combine the strictly utilitarian – kitchen chairs and draughtsman's stool – and the homely, like the old wooden storage trunk.

OPPOSITE: Pieces of professional office furniture – an ergonomically designed Eames chair and a matt black filing cabinet, for example – are in interesting contrast to, and balanced by, the rough, untreated planks of wood used on the wall.

A desk or work surface does not have to be hidden away, pushed against a wall, or try to be invisible. A well-designed piece like this desk – 'Pablo' by Porada – is positioned boldly, looking out into the room, a highly desirable object in its own right.

RIGHT and FAR RIGHT: Even the smallest corner of a room can be converted, in the simplest of ways, into an effective work space; like a chameleon, this desk can turn in a moment from work station to part of a decorative corner within the larger room. Behind the table top, an attractive, semi-opaque blind that works with the general decor can be easily drawn down, thus hiding the equipment and files stored on the shelves behind.

with the luxury of more space than you need. Think about exactly what you might need and how you would use it. You may, after all, not need any traditional office furniture at all. Much of it is not particularly good looking and certainly most of it seems to have been designed by someone more interested in robotic, metal uniformity than whether it might give any sort of visual pleasure. You may even have exactly what you need already – although you have not yet realized it.

Perhaps you are not thinking in terms of offices at all, but rather more of a creative work space, where you can work on projects for your own business, or simply for yourself – somewhere where you can keep and store,

in organized, orderly fashion, all the tools of your trade, art or craft, without having to move everything every evening when family life intrudes. Often, the aesthetic pleasure of a room comes not from additional decorative touches but from the tools of the trade – the skeins of wool, jars of paint or rolls of fabric.

Or the space may be somewhere you can happily pursue those relaxing pastimes still occasionally, and somewhat patronizingly, called hobbies, where you can keep together the references, information and tools required for your particular enthusiasm.

It doesn't matter; what does matter is that, somewhere in your home, there is a space that is strictly and utterly for you. Now read on.

the elements

A double work space designed in the simplest, most functional way: a desk that is almost rough-hewn faces a window, below which are bookshelves. Everything else is reduced back to its quietest form – white paint, slatted wooden panelling and polished wooden floor. No decorative ornaments intrude on the sense of calm.

RIGHT: A space with a distinct purpose – somewhere to meet, to plan, to discuss. The absence of any distracting clutter around the white space, the abundance of natural light and the pale calm colour of both walls and furniture make this a space for serious work.

FURNITURE & SPACE

The simple fact is that almost everyone can carve out some sort of space of their own at home; after all, a desk and a brace of shelves rather than the kitchen table must surely be within almost everyone's grasp. You've got the computer or laptop, you've got the phone – now, where can you set yourself up relatively undisturbed? No matter how simple or small the area, you will almost immediately notice the difference that it will make to your life having even a mini-space that is your own. In a moment you will find yourself more productive, more organized, even more creative.

So this is a room that can not only be justified in terms of practicality – somewhere to do the family

23

A generous-sized antique pine kitchen table – with its deep cutlery drawers and shelf below perfect for storage – makes an effective workspace, and looks great coupled with the individual, quirky chair.

OPPOSITE: Not, at first sight, a conventional office space, this is a very personal spot, and somewhere which has actually been thought out with care. At the top of a staircase, a table, a chair, a light, sharpened pencils and a notebook are ready for action.

finances or run a business – but which is also enormously satisfying on a personal level. One of the many appealing aspects of working from home is that you have control over how your space is designed, and the ability to move away from the conventional idea of how an office should look; instead, you can design and furnish it how you would like it to be – often, no always, a very different matter.

OPPOSITE AND LEFT: Two simple set-ups that show how easy it is to use what is readily available and to hand to create calm working spaces that are fit for purpose. Old and antique pine kitchen tables, sometimes painted, sometimes worn to a comfortable patina, have integral drawers that make perfect hold-alls for stationery and necessities. Traditional wooden kitchen chairs eased with plump cushions are ergonomic without knowing it.

BELOW: The rather sculptural 'Yves' writing desk, by Russel Pinch, is beautifully designed: it is light and delicate with an integral stationery compartment and a raised section holding everything, including an angled light, to leave the desk space free of encumbrance.

Peace and quiet are as important as seating and storage

This is the moment to bring in ergonomics – a word much bandied about and most often used to show that the speaker or writer has a working knowledge of the principles of office, or kitchen, design. In its broadest sense, it can probably be defined as the art or science of

A fine example of design that works, this is a space that can disappear into the wall when not required. A hinged panel that folds down to reveal a desk surface and comprehensive filing system that is otherwise hidden from view. Above, deep shelves hold all other necessary equipment and files.

LEFT: A discreet and beautifully planned working area with deep shelves, surfaces that slide silently way, and a swivel chair that would not look out of place in a bedroom.

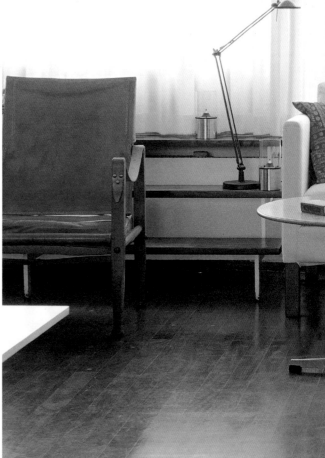

designing pieces of equipment that are suitable for their purpose, and then combining such pieces to most efficient advantage. You could argue that there is nothing new about this. After all, a good breakfront Georgian desk is perfectly designed to suit the user; built at a height that allows comfortable, relaxed posture and with shelves and drawers set close at hand and ready for writing.

Today, though, the look of a piece of
furniture sometimes seems more important
than its purpose – as anyone who has suffered
back or joint pain at the office will testify.
Your own home version of ergonomically
designed work space, therefore, should
ensure that both the work surface and chair
are at the right height to support you, and
that all the things that you will need are
close at hand and can be reached with ease.

Remember that the components of a home office should be there to suit you, not vice versa, and that, rather like the 'golden triangle' of a kitchen where preparation, cooking and storage areas – that is to say, sink, stovetop and refrigerator/freezer – are all linked together within comfortable striking distance, so your working area should be similarly planned.

When planning your home space, it is helpful to make a flexible wish list: not only the basic things you know you will need – a work surface, a chair and somewhere to store things – but also the things you would really like to have in this most personal of spaces. And as with all interior design, remember that once you get the basics – the bones – right, the rest

Choose to have around you things that you really like in this most personal of spaces

OPPOSITE: In a wider context, it is often good to design your private space as part of a greater design whole. In this studio, a long, white-painted draughtsman's trestle table is matched with a 20th century classic chair, and placed against a wall beneath a striking painting, the tones of which are echoed in the oversized floor lamp. A large container of flowers and decorative objects beneath the painting emphasize that design is as important as function.

ABOVE RIGHT: Extremely fit for purpose is this fine antique roll-top desk which needs no further embellishment other than a tall desk lamp and a comfortable chair in which to relax.

BELOW RIGHT: An old, white-painted bureau desk is a compact office in itself, with its upper cupboard in which to store large files and its assortment of small shallow drawers which are essential in any efficient office.

Ensure that the height of both desk and chair are right for
your specific needs and type of work

will fall into place with relative ease.

Addressing your needs – which may be
very different to the next person and very
different to the way you may have worked
in a commercial office – is the first priority.
First of all, this is a space where you can
think along alternative lines – rather than
thinking of your needs as a desk and shelves,

consider what you truly need in spacial terms
– probably a flat, deep surface at one level,
other flat surfaces at higher levels and some
sort of containers for storage.

As far as the basics go, a desktop or work
surface is perhaps the easiest element to get
right; the most important thing here being
that – whether you are contemplating a state

OPPOSITE: A free-standing desk or table must have enough room on it to house all the pieces of office equipment that you will need, from a telephone to a computer as well as an adjustable light.

RIGHT: Not all specifically designed office chairs are utilitarian and dull. Some light research will reveal that there are some really good looking designs available that are both stylish and protective of your back and spine.

of the art, custom-made desk, or thinking of using an old table that is already kicking around – the height must be right for your particular needs and type of work.

And, of course, your chair must also be suitable. It is very tempting to just use a chair that is already there, or that is particularly attractive; the fact is that if you spend any amount of time sitting in one place, it is far better to have a chair that has been designed for the job. Sitting down for a long time isn't particularly natural or good for you and so you need a chair that supports your spine – in particular your lower back, the source of so many aches and pains.

The style of the furniture that you choose is obviously dictated by your personal taste and also by the style and design of your home. A classic desk, specially designed for the purpose, which is either antique or new is the ultimate functional luxury. Such pieces

HOW TO ENSURE OFFICE COMFORT

* In a perfect world your desk height should be 65–70 cm (26–28 inches) from the floor, more so if you are taller.

* Your elbows should be able to rest at a 90° angle on the surface.

* Your chair should be between 40–50 cm (16–20 inches) from the floor.

* Thighs should be horizontal and feet flat on the ground.

* Your back should touch the back of the chair, and your arms rest comfortably on the work surface.

* Look for a swivelling, adjustable chair with lumbar support.

* Your work should be within a comfortable field of vision – less than 64 cm (25 inches) from the eyes.

will slide easily into a larger scheme and so are ideal if your space is not self-contained. If, on the other hand, you have an entire room to play with, then obviously anything goes, governed only by your taste and your pocket; here, your dream desk might be anything from an antique refectory table or a door turned upside down and balanced on small filing cabinets, to a state-of-the-art elliptical or L-shaped office centre.

If you decide on a relatively conventional office layout, there are numerous companies and stores which offer variants on the theme, and at every price level. Just as there are fitted kitchen and bedroom furniture ranges, there are fitted office systems too. If this is the direction you want to take, think about what combination of shelving, drawers and desktops you would need. Again, as with kitchens, it is all too easy to be blinded or confused by the choice available, so familiarize yourself before you sally out to spend: go into office

ABOVE, LEFT AND RIGHT: the 'Covet' desk by Case is an excellent example of contemporary work space design; it not only allows enough room to work comfortably, but also has the ability to easily become, when work equipment is removed, an occasional or dining table. Invisible, shallow drawers built into the frame and the storage trough between the trestles are an integral part of the whole design.

OPPOSITE: The simplest of office systems, 'Portus Walnut', by Russell Pinch, incorporates a made-for-purpose desk with both deep and shallow drawers as well as a generous work surface. It is paired with a wall-hung storage unit with both open and closed adaptable compartments.

Industrial furniture is often well-suited to home office use, with its functional and funky air. Here a metal work table is combined with an early swivel chair to great effect.

OPPOSITE: A lightweight, airy, almost fragile work table, paired with a rather sturdier looking adjustable chair makes for an interesting combination of styles.

showrooms, look at brochures or on the internet to see what you are drawn to and what might work for you, before you invest.

Where to find the furniture you need is a road with many interesting byways and alleys. If you feel slightly dejected at the idea of travelling the conventional office furniture route, think a little laterally and consider recycling in its broadest sense. The original recyclers, long before it became a lifestyle option, were, of course, antique dealers, and antique shops and fairs are still marvellous treasure troves to be explored. Not quite so romantic perhaps, but equally fertile grounds are second-hand furniture shops – including the sort that sell on furniture clearance goods and where the pavement acts as an alfresco showroom. Be selective and be imaginative – a rubbish looking, but solid wooden desk in a junk shop, that happens to have a large enough work surface and good-sized drawers, might look completely different painted in a good colour, and with shiny new handles.

Other interesting sources might include car boot and attic sales, or the internet. Look for the websites devoted to connecting people who want to get rid of unwanted items for little or no money, such as one of the swapping sites, or sites like freecycle (www.freecycle.org), where unwanted goods can be posted and also discovered. The more you put into the search for the perfect pieces, the more fun it will all become.

Think laterally when looking for work space furniture. Often the most unpromising sources can yield up rich pickings

STORAGE & SHELVING

A certain amount of storage is essential but it doesn't have to come as a matching set. Use contrasting textures and styles, mixing free-standing units with wooden shelving and basket-work open boxes.

OPPOSITE: Rejuvenated office pieces, like this newly painted plan chest and brightly upholstered chair, have all the advantages of purpose-built efficiency coupled with a touch of unique originality.

Storage, as a concept, has several functions: it keeps the area around you – particularly the floors and flat surfaces – free of clutter; it is also a way of arranging the things that you need to hand in an intelligent and functional way so that you can find anything necessary, at any time, with ease. One of the unwritten laws of storage is that you always have more things to store than you originally envisaged, including all those things that have been half-forgotten – possibly because, over time, they have been pushed, metaphorically, beneath and behind things. So since good storage requires logic and thought, take some time identifying not only what exactly you want to store in this space, but how and where you want to store it.

The next thing is to try and work out how to keep to a minimum the things that need storing – particularly paperwork for, no matter how much talk there is about the paperless office, there often seems to be just as much as there ever was – sometimes, even more.

For what it's worth, my personal, completely unscientific, de-clutter regime (which I try to do first thing in the morning) is to take any accumulated

A well-designed storage unit is a pleasure to behold particularly when, like the one shown here, each section is designed with a particular purpose in mind.

OPPOSITE: Even if you have room for nothing more elaborate, build an endlessly adaptable shelf, or two, or three into your work area, anywhere there is room. Decorative interest has been added by using the same design of coloured storage boxes, in different sizes, to make pleasing groups.

papers and letters, as well as a pen, paper, diary and bill-paying equipment, and go through them sorting them into 'bin', 'save', and 'act on' piles. If it's a bill, pay it. If it's an invitation, letter, card or enquiry, answer it – either by e-mail, telephone or letter. Once a week (on Monday mornings, if I'm organized), I go through the 'save' and 'act on' piles again and take any further action. As I say, it's not very scientific, but for me it keeps everything manageable and keeps me more or less in control.

For more permanent storage, the ideal is to have everything on hand, with necessities in view and all else hidden away. We all have things that we would prefer not to see around us: personally, I do not find computers and all their attendant paraphernalia attractive, and I like all the equipment that I use to be as hidden as possible,

ABOVE LEFT: Industrial and domestic trolleys are available in many sizes, shapes, and materials and almost all of them can be used to great manoeuvrable advantage in a work space.

ABOVE RIGHT: Sectioned storage, designed to hold large box files, will keep a paper-hungry office space both neat and good looking.

OPPOSITE LEFT: A salvaged wire-mesh plant rack holds everything from books and papers to pictures and decorative geegaws.

OPPOSITE RIGHT: Plywood or cardboard magazine holders, when bought in quantity, are a fail-safe way of keeping stray books and papers in order.

FILING GUIDELINES: WHAT YOU NEED TO KEEP AND FOR HOW LONG

* You should keep all long-term official papers – title deeds, insurance policies and so on.

* Then there is money. Keep bank, credit card and building society statements for at least six years, as well as all correspondence between you and your bank appertaining to your accounts and deposits.

* There is a legal requirement to keep documents appertaining to tax returns for a certain amount of time: check with the revenue service of your country of domicile for guidelines. Such documents would include dividend certificates and pay slips. As far as this category goes, the mantra should be – if in doubt, don't throw it out.

* Keep all certificates relating to your family records. Birth, marriage, divorce and death should all be kept; it is extremely time-consuming, expensive and sometimes distressing to have to get replacement copies of these. Also important medical information should be close to hand.

* Your children will thank you – eventually – for keeping school reports, and childhood certificates for achievements in sports, swimming, music and so on.

* A metal, fire-proof box is an easy, and portable if necessary, way to keep all these important records close at hand.

with the printer on a deep, lower shelf where it can sit
humming happily unseen by me, and the modem tucked
into a space beneath the worktop.

For many people, a wall of storage is the ultimate
answer to all these problems – in a perfect world,
perhaps a custom-built wall of cupboards to conceal,
and a set of shelves to display. Although the grandest

A large, but almost industrial like working space, which draws on the simplicity of warehouse storage units and is fitted with a ceiling-high wall of metal shelving. Large industrial boxes that continue the utilitarian theme are stacked in serious rows.

OPPOSITE TOP RIGHT: A retro, compact working space; a neat, vintage desk and an ex-postal sorting cabinet, equipped with enough compartments and cubicles for every piece of paper to be filed with ease.

OPPOSITE FAR LEFT: A two-person desk system with the space admirably arranged for maximum efficiency and adaptable storage. Particularly noteworthy is an eye-level shelving system with sliding panels which can conceal or reveal as required, and a useful end-wall open storage unit can be accessed from either side.

OPPOSITE BELOW RIGHT: Simple, inexpensive and efficient – a small corner working space which is delineated by a half-height narrow filing cabinet beside a simple worktop, with, above, two shelves on brackets; this simple arrangement is augmented by a quantity of plywood and wicker containers.

examples might be expensive, even a set of simple shelves covering as much wall space as possible can make a huge difference; for without shelving for books, boxes, baskets, files, you will never achieve any sense of order or organization. Whether you are doing your own thing or running a business, without organization, all else will be in vain. Even a single shelf

A working space that has benefited from much careful thought and planning to make the most of what is ultimately a very small working area. On one wall, floor-to-ceiling open shelves have been installed, the perfect answer for universal storage. On the other side of the window, a two-tiered semi-circular desk unit has been installed, making the best use of what would otherwise be a tight space.

OPPOSITE: Easy to achieve, good looking and efficient: floor to ceiling wooden open shelving with enough space for everything to be stored either on view or ranged in open boxes.

OPPOSITE: Rescued and recycled, the shelving is made from reclaimed railway sleepers and coupled with wooden crates for extra storage.

ABOVE LEFT: On a shelf below the work space, mis-matched bags and boxes used as storage vessels add interest.

ABOVE RIGHT: A small alcove is used for a recessed set of book shelves that sit conveniently close to a built-in work surface.

RIGHT: A metallic exercise – an antique table coupled with a metal filing cabinet and chair. Even the pictures and radiator are finished in the same tones.

on simple brackets will make a difference, and a set of shelves, on adjustable brackets, will change your life.

Of course shelving does not have to be built in: it can be a piece of furniture – a small (or large) bookcase adapted to hold more than books. It can be on castors so that it can be moved around according to whim or need. It can be wall hung, or it can be free standing; it can be cheap or it can be expensive. One of the most useful of storage

LEFT: At the top of the house, a beamed attic room has been made into a working space that is functional and utilitarian, but none the worse for that. The very practicality of the solid work bench, the industrial shelving and the neatly ranged box files, coupled with the solid filing cabinets ranged along the walls, make the whole space pleasing in the extreme.

OPPOSITE: A writer's dream: acres of shelving with room for every reference and inspirational book that you could ever ask for, coupled with a long – very long – writing table where papers and files can pile up ad nauseam.

For many people a wall of shelving, in whatever form, is the ultimate solution to the storage problem

systems is the traditional bookcase design – shelves above, deeper cupboards below.

Even with the best set of shelves, you will probably still need something in which to file papers. Although filing cabinets are undeniably useful, they are not by their nature, objects of beauty. If you cannot live without them, consider a scaled down pair to sit beneath the desk top, or even to act as supports for a work surface. Metal cabinets

can be sprayed almost any colour as well as being re-invigorated with wall- or wrapping paper, or even fabric-covered fronts.

In addition, look for unusual hooks and pegs – from butchers hooks to coat racks. Pieces designed as kitchen storage may work in your craft space; ditto laundry and bathroom storage, which are designed to fit into the tightest of spaces and may just fit your particular bill.

case study

Mark Smith, an interior designer based in London, believes in the power of functional, good looking storage that comes without a designer price tag.

In Mark's carefully designed, but simple office, a heavy wood and melamine double desktop rests on a group of white filing cabinets, arranged so that they are accessible both at desk side as well as room side. On wooden shelves set into an alcove, matt perspex box files hold books and papers, whilst on the shelf below, magazines are kept in check with the same box files displayed with their low backs to the room for easy access. A simple stack of clear plastic boxes, similar to those found in craft shops, is a perfect repository for everything from staples to rubber bands and paper clips.

ABOVE: Behind one side of the double desk, in the alcove beside the fireplace, deep shelves have been inset where all files, books and magazines can be kept in perfect order.

RIGHT: A set of shallow clear plastic boxes, available from office suppliers, craft and DIY shops, hold small pieces and look good enough to keep on permanent display.

OPPOSITE: Pared-down chic is only attainable when every piece is considered on design merits as well as functionality. From the brave chrome task light to the printer and pencil pot, nothing jars the eye.

TASK LIGHTING

Although light, and therefore lighting, is a fundamental need of man, the way that we utilize lighting is very different now to the way it was for hundreds of years when the choice was limited to dark or light, bright or dim. It is amusing to recall that when electricity was first introduced into wealthy households, society ladies were outraged by the revealing effect that such bright light had on their previously mysterious, shaded beauty.

Now, of course, we realize that good lighting is integral to the success of a room. It is also – and this is relevant when discussing a creative space of your own – integral to the way you feel. Bad

OPPOSITE: A pair of vintage, adjustable lights sit either end of the work table, whilst a dropped ceiling light gives overall ambient illumination.

BELOW LEFT: A clip-on, adjustable angled light has the double advantage of practicality and adaptability. Finished in go-with-everything, metallic grey, it is as much at home in a decorative display as it is at the edge of a desk.

BELOW RIGHT: With its heavy base and oversized metal shade, this semi-industrial lamp is almost a design statement in its own right, as well of course, as being totally functional.

lighting, lighting under which you strain to see what you are doing, can – literally – make you feel ill. Good lighting, on the other hand, sympathetically positioned and offering light where it is needed, will make you feel both positive and even stimulated.

Lighting today is a complex and diverse area; we have moved far away from the idea of a single central light source – at its simplest, the overhead ceiling light – augmented with a couple of standard or table lights. Instead, lighting is sophisticated, complex and often very beautiful, and there are designs and schemes for every possible situation and room, including your own particular needs and wants.

As with everything else that is important in your own space, the lighting that you will need for your work will depend firstly on whether your space is a part of a larger area or whether it is a room

ABOVE LEFT: Worthy of an old-fashioned newspaper office ready to 'hold the front page', a wooden traditional desk and assorted files and drawers are illuminated by a metal desk lamp that fits perfectly with its surroundings.

ABOVE RIGHT: Daylight is discreetly filtered through a sheer roll-up blind – a silk fabric of banana leaf design by Andrew Martin – that is raised and lowered with a contrasting ribbon tie, whilst a traditional, classic metal desk lamp is used for close-up work.

Lit by a large window, through which daylight pours, this comfortable study is almost self-consciously set in the middle of the last century – at the very latest. A sturdy Bakelite telephone, an ink bottle and pens are arranged on the desk, while a tall adjustable light sits to one side. Brass rails create a storage space for smaller items and a rush-seated chair completes the picture. But, partially hidden from this timeless scene, a computer screen lurks behind a small built-in bookcase, and discreet cupboards below doubtless conceal further evidence of contemporary working life.

There is enough natural light in this room to eliminate the necessity for a specific task light. Ambient lighting need not be utilitarian – here it is provided in the form of a delicate tear-drop chandelier, which uses candles to illuminate the room.

OPPOSITE: Carefully chosen wall lights can work very well, freeing up valuable desk space. In a house by the sea, this particular pair of lights look as though they have been made from pieces of driftwood, and have shades of straw, garnished with small bucolic straw tufts at intervals.

on its own; and secondly on what tasks or work you intend to pursue. It is usually important that there is a variety of light sources with a mixture of ambient and background lighting in place – using different qualities of light – all acting as back-up to the all-important specific task lighting. Different tasks require different types of lighting; if you are working at a desk, for example, good lighting is just as – if not more – important as the desk or chair, and if you are doing close work of any kind, from painting to metalwork, several different targeted lights might be necessary.

It is important that there should be a variety of light sources that combine a mixture of ambient and specific lighting

So, before you decide what you need, make a list of what precisely you will be doing in this space – might you be reading, and writing, and perhaps doing fine craft work, and if so, will you need different types of lighting for each activity?

If you have natural light, you start at an advantage. Natural light is the best thing that you can have to work by, so study it – not just how much there is, or how large the window or windows that will illuminate your work space are, but also which direction the window faces, whether the light is warm or cold and whether it lasts all day. If you have a choice, position your work space as close to the natural light source as you are able.

There is plenty of natural light here, which is filtered when necessary by slatted venetian blinds, and augmented by an all-purpose, angled light which fastens to the edge of the desk and can be directed wherever task lighting is most needed.

Remember though, that however good it may be, and although there cannot be too much of it, natural light will still always need to be augmented by artificial lighting, even if only for dark days and evening work. You will also very probably need a blind or blinds in order to regulate and control direct sunlight, and do ensure that the desk can be positioned so that direct light does not fall on the computer screen.

For close work, task lighting is usually best if it is a directional light that can be manoeuvred to illuminate different areas. The lighting should be situated so that it does not throw a shadow over your work. There are too many light designs to list here, although for many artists and writers, the traditional lines of an angled work light remain the preferred solution, with the Anglepoise being the classic design. First produced in 1933 by George Cawardine, the workings of the Anglepoise were designed to imitate the joints of a human arm. It has inspired many contemporary versions, many beautiful as well as functional. Increasingly also, designers are producing specific lighting designs that are intended to work

In this work room, close-up lighting is needed over the centre work-table area. The original and alternative solution has been to suspend an oversized industrial lamp, which operates on a hook and pulley system. Attached to a winch, the light can be lowered or raised at will.

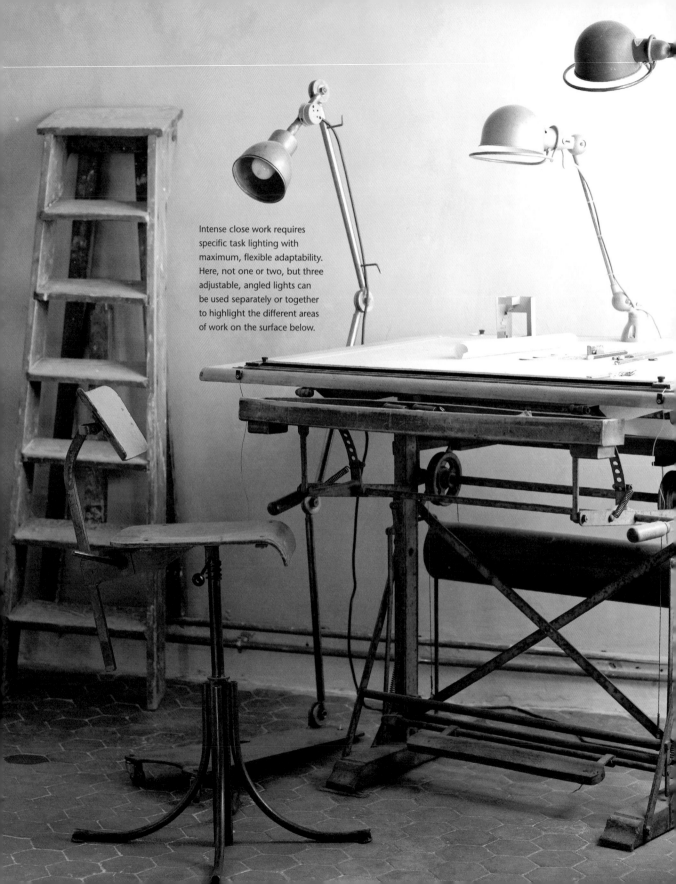

Intense close work requires specific task lighting with maximum, flexible adaptability. Here, not one or two, but three adjustable, angled lights can be used separately or together to highlight the different areas of work on the surface below.

Where two or more people work together, it is essential to have a enough lights for all. Relatively inexpensive, and 6lights such as these can make a simple space feel luxurious.

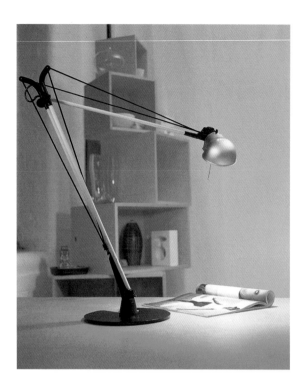

LEFT: Loosely based on the concept of the 20th century adjustable, angled lamp, this modern lamp from Babylon Design is a fascinating combination of almost ethereal fragility, combined with precision engineering and electronic expertise.

RIGHT: A floor lamp of almost natural beauty by Babylon Design is combined in this work space, with a clutch of other lamps of different heights and functions giving maximum flexibility to the work space.

Look for contemporary versions of the original Anglepoise lamp – a design that is both beautiful and functional

in tandem with a desktop computer – being of traditional desk-lamp height but with a swivelling, narrow, elliptical canopy that distributes light across the whole screen.

Wall-mounted lights, particularly if they are directional or angled, are another way to illuminate a specific space or place, and can free up desk space. If there are shelves above

your work surface, consider some of the designs intended as kitchen down lighters; indeed, do not scorn ranges intended for kitchens or bedrooms – wall mounted swing-armed bedroom reading lamps are functional and very adaptable, too.

For spaces which lack wider access to electricity, there are now work lamps, both desk-based and and floor-standing, which are solar powered – ideal for a space which benefits from an abundance of natural light, or a garden studio.

And remember that whilst the main emphasis should be on task lighting, it is pleasant, in your personal space, to have some lights that are just enjoyable – they may be decorative, or quirky, or icons of contemporary design: mix them in and find places where their assets will be appreciated. It all makes for a perfect room of your own.

DECORATION

Whether your space is a separate room or part of a larger area, it is important to decorate it in a way that not only acts as a demarcation of the subtlest kind, but that will also help to inspire you when you are working. Do not stint on its adornment – which of course is not at all the same thing as saying do not stint on how much you spend on it. But a work space should – no, must – be somewhere that is inspiring, and the more that it is decorated in a way that pleases you – really pleases you – the more inspired you will be. Pictures, for example; would it not be nice to put the picture that you love most on the wall where you work every day? For that matter, what about creating a mini-gallery of pictures hung around you? And the piece of china that you inherited from your granny, and which has no particular significance for anyone else, should that not be on a shelf close by? For although this is a working space, it is also the place where some of your dearest things should be, along with all those favourite postcards, books and other things that bring you cheer.

Obviously the colours that you choose for your space are central to your well-being. Even if this is to be a home office rather than a craft space, there is no need at all to stay with the neutral colour palette beloved by office managers and designers all over the business world. You may be someone who responds to bright, vibrant colours that stimulate you, and excite and inspire; or you may instead be someone who prefers calm, contemplative colours to allow your inner creativity to peacefully emerge. And colour

A simple idea, but an effective one. On the wall behind the work table, and therefore close to hand, is strung, from end to end, a line, across which all manner of objects both useful and decorative have been hung.

OPPOSITE: A mini-symphony in white, with a particularly glamorous chrome and white leather chair, this simple but harmonious space employs a panel of strongly patterned wallpaper to disguise the otherwise boring space behind the desk, on the grounds of a little of what you fancy does you good!

Although this is a working space,
it is where some of your dearest
possessions should be

In a corner of a minimalist, white-painted room, the wall behind this trestle desk has become a veritable inspiration and memory board, covered as it is with children's drawings, sketches, postcards and even impressions of small hand- and footprints.

OPPOSITE: Making this work table a self-contained, personal space has been imaginatively achieved by creating an inspiration wall above the desk, including everything from pretty postcards to fabric swatches. To the side, a bright curtain is used to conceal shelves full of files.

shouldn't just be on walls – think about using colour on furniture – a simple way of transforming what was once a standard table, or boring chest of drawers. Paint is the easy, and possibly first option; but think also of using textiles to brighten up spaces in awkward corners or under the stairs: not necessarily a piece of furnishing fabric, but something that inspires you – a length of dress fabric, a bright, fringed silk shawl, sari

OPPOSITE: This well-organized study has all the advantages you could want when working on your own. A comfortable, large desk with good adjustable lighting and adequate storage; an ideas wall crammed with sketches, drawings and photographs to inspire, and best of all, a window that looks out onto a constantly changing garden view.

RIGHT: For many people, being able to work in a garden room is the absolute best possible situation in which to find themselves. Close to, but also far from, domestic life, with all the advantages that such an arrangement brings, with the added pleasure of looking out onto the beautiful, ever-changing, and always inspirational landscape.

silk or an oversized leopard printed scarf.

It is fun to use dual purpose containers for the inevitable bits and pieces that are part of any working space. Favourite jugs of different sizes to hold pens, pencils, brushes and so on. Chateau-stamped wooden claret and burgundy wine boxes, which look great

If you have a garden as a view, you need little else in the way of visual diversion

and hold a lot of stuff. Decorative boxes – wood, china, metal – for small stationery pieces. And find a place for phones – both hand-sets and mobiles; convenient though it is to no longer have to have a dedicated phone-jack or line within an office space, it does make sense to have some sort of open container for phones, for it is all too easy to lose them dramatically beneath the papers covering the worktop. An open box, a decorative mug, some type of container in which you can stand them, meerkat-style, will save you many annoying minutes of futile scrabbling whilst they plaintively ring.

case study

Neisha Crosland is one of the most influential textile designers working today. In her airy, period London house, a large room dominated by windows serves as her creative base.

Neisha is a master, or rather mistress, of flat pattern – a textile designer who extends her remit into so much else, textiles yes, but also everything from cushions to wallpapers, stationery, rugs, tiles and even the odd handbag. She admits to being a tidy person and much of her inspiration comes from nature's designs, liking as she does, 'the way nature arranges itself on leaves, petals and stamens.' In her home, rather than a conventional inspiration board in front of a desk, she has instead a floor-length mirror behind her chair, the tall frame of which is entirely covered with things to inspire and remind, from postcards of favourite paintings to fragments of antique textiles and scraps of sundry patterns and designs which appeal to her. Not only does it act as inspiration, it also is part of the cool, calm presence of everything in this sunny, simple room.

THIS PAGE AND OPPOSITE:
In Neisha Crosland's creative
base, daylight, tempered by
adjustable sheer Roman
blinds, floods the room.
Although there are
inspirational triggers
everywhere to be seen, there
is an order in their
arrangement: the full-sized
mirror leaning against the
wall behind the desk acts
as a giant frame for an
assortment of cards and, at
eye-level, above a set of low
cupboards is a pleasingly
arranged group of pictures.

LEFT: Extremely stylish and sophisticated, yet also functional and very efficient, this home office is dominated by the beautifully designed and comprehensive wall storage system with a place for everything and where everything is in its place.

ABOVE: A busy home office in a corner has been set up in a classic L-shape, which is the most efficient of office layouts in that it provides both enough storage close to hand as well as flexible and comprehensive working space.

HOME OFFICES

Although the home office is becoming almost as much of a cliché as that of the kitchen being the heart of the home, the huge growth in internet use, as well as the resulting increase in technological paraphernalia, does mean that the way we organize our lives at home has changed enormously. In most homes, space needs to be

77

A raised dais is a perfect setting for a contemporary home office – from the full-height plate glass windows overlooking a spectacular panoramic view of Los Angeles, to the desk that is long enough to take in that view, and with one chair for action, and another for thought. Add to that copious shelving and state-of-the art directional lamps; result – an office from which to rule the world.

In one corner of a home office, a full-length blind controls and diffuses the daylight that floods this L-shaped work area. The functional elements of the work set-up are softened by just the right percentage of decorative objects, coupled with the aesthetic pleasure of a wide-bladed ceiling fan and a low hanging lamp.

OPPOSITE: A symphony in wood, this office arrangement of polished wooden desk and free-standing cabinet nods to mid-20th century Scandinavian design. The clean lines and uncluttered surfaces are as attractive and practical today as when they were first designed.

set aside for a computer, through which we will order all manner of goods and services from the internet. In addition, we pay bills over the phone, run our bank accounts, and book holidays, and all these are transactions which need recording, complete with contact numbers and references. So even though our lives are meant to be easier, and of course in many ways they are, some sort of dedicated home office space is really almost essential.

In this chapter we will assume that you are lucky enough to be able to find, somewhere in your home, a whole room in which you can install yourself. A room of one's own, as Virginia Woolf named it, a place that is wholly for oneself, that is luck indeed, no matter how small the space. For, funnily

Carefully planned rooms, complete with filing cabinets, desks and computers, make work a total pleasure

enough, it is not a question of size, in fact many would posit that a small space is even better than a large one as it becomes, at once, identifiably one's own without much work; and traditionally, the study was always an intimate space – a place where everything you needed and wanted was immediately to hand behind the satisfyingly closed door.

The best room for a home office is a room that is presently unused, but today, other than

This fine example of a study is arranged so comfortably and stylishly, in every way, from the classic lines of the lamp to the chair and lacquered black desk. There is no sense of office, with all the dry connotations such a word brings.

The secret of a good office at home is to combine comfort, multi-purpose furniture and stylish storage with carefully chosen decorative bits so that no one piece or element looks out of place with anything else in the room. The cat is optional.

case study

Although perfection is never easy to achieve, this working space, a home office made for two – Ingrid and Avinash Persuad – comes pretty close to getting there.

Bright, open and airy, with sunlight flooding the room, the clever design and well-planned storage of this contemporary home office mean that two can work as comfortably as one. The work-induced clutter that can so easily accrue when two people work alongside each other is minimized here with the installation of pull-down blinds, hiding untidy but essential paraphernalia.

ABOVE: Copious shelving – both deep and wide – means that reference books can be stored in a manner that keeps them both organized and to hand.

RIGHT: An almost sculptural composition of a wall of nine clocks above two classic Eames rocking chairs combines both adequate seating and an element of visual satisfaction.

A continuous work surface, long enough to seat two people, has desk-level storage that can be closed off, as well as, above the desktop, open shelves for instant access. To one side, deep alcove shelving holds matching box files.

in an old, rambling house, such a find is rarely on the cards. So it is necessary to either commandeer an existing room, or make a new room where none was before.

If commandeering is going to be done, the obvious choice for most people would be a guest or spare bedroom: positioned within the body of the house, with existing electricity and heating, and a door that – presumably – closes. What could be more perfect? Well not much, except for those people who may wish to continue to use it for its original purpose, and to think of it as primarily a bedroom. This will not do; if you do decide that this would be the right room for you,

ABOVE: A perfect example of a room that has been designed specifically to fit its owner's personality: a sense of order and scale prevail here, along with a feeling of precision and control.

OPPOSITE: Quirky and individual, this working area has everything to hand, much of it stored in an alternative way, with wooden crates and boxes being used for the storage of large books and unwieldy objects.

then a half-hearted conversion will not work. Either just get rid of the bed and let them find somewhere else to stay, or divide off the working part of the room with curtains, screens, or furniture and install a handsome but discreet filing and storage system where your work, papers and so on can be kept when the room is in guest mode. And you

might consider investing in a good sofabed, which will give your working room a far more professional aspect.

It is quite likely that the space – the actual room – is physically not there and a suitable space must be identified, investigated and probably transformed. It could be an attic or loft space, large enough to stand up in, that can be converted relatively reasonably, or perhaps even a junk-room or basement, which has never before been used for living; or even a garage that might be commandeered at not too great a cost.

In many ways, a loft or attic is almost the ideal home office, as its location, at the top

The more of your own things that you have around you, the more comfortable you will feel

of the house, means that it will be relatively quiet and cut off from family noise and activity. Some loft spaces are better than others – windows are important, and the higher the ceiling, the better. Although you might well be able to do the conversion

OPPOSITE: In the tradition of studies as a room where the owner's favourite things were kept, this is the study of a true modern-day collector, filled with unusual objects – some valuable, some rare, all interesting. Everything has been given a place and displayed to best advantage.

ABOVE: In just one corner of the room, there are things to look at on every level, from the Arts and Crafts wooden chair to the leather-bound books and early photographs. Although they are all very different in scale, together they form a harmonious composition.

conversion may well not need planning permission, it is extremely important to find out what building regulations might apply and whether you will need to strengthen the flooring, for example.

Moving downwards into a basement or under-street space is another option; again planning permission is not normally required unless you are adding external doors and windows, but it is of course wise to check first. Ventilation, insulation and damp-proofing are, however, essentials, as is, in many cases, efficient air-conditioning, and all these requirements may call for professional advice, as well as the services of a specialist basement conversion company –

If your home office can be situated somewhere quiet and removed from household noise, so much the better

yourself, if it has been used as a room at sometime in the past, consider having it fitted out professionally by a joiner who can make the most of any awkward angles and make use of every inch of space, particularly for clever storage. And although a loft

ABOVE: In a corner of a sunny area at the top of the house, clever planning and cabinet work has provided everything that is needed for a simple but perfect work space. White-painted woodwork – including the floor – makes the area look large and commodious.

OPPOSITE: In an airy corner of a space beneath the roof, a small but perfectly formed working area has been carved out of what once was part of a factory, where the desk lighting hangs from the original pulley system. There is just enough room for a table and chair, and French windows and pretty inner glass doors maximize the available natural light.

OPPOSITE: No matter how simple, any space can be fitted with shelves; in many cases they are all that you need to create an instant work space that fulfils on every level. On the lowest level, uprights divide the shelves into convenient compartments for smaller storage in this charasmatic and inviting space.

RIGHT: Although beautiful to look at, this period window takes up most of the outside wall, so storage space must be found wherever possible. The solution here has been to build shelves that reach all the way up to the high ceiling, and make higher shelves accessible with the help of a tapered library ladder. A desk and chair are positioned to catch the natural light from the window.

usually a wise move, when plans are radical.

The relative weather-worthiness of modern cars means another possible work space is the garage, which more often than not seems, these days, to be used as a repository for extra junk – sorry, important, unused belongings. To convert part, if not all, of a garage space into an office or crafts room – particularly if you have large pieces of equipment – can make both physical and economic sense. Converting the whole garage might mean that there will be a certain amount of initial administrative work to be done, such as

finding out whether there are any restrictive clauses in your deeds about making such changes; and finding out if planning permission would be required were you to add windows or change doors. But, in many cases, such a transformation would be comparatively plain sailing.

Working in a garden office – otherwise known as 'just going to the shed' – is a new and increasingly popular way of making a really useful space out of what, in many cases, was originally nothing at all. But be warned, a regular shed, in the traditional, Mr

Simplicity is always the best policy: here, a long wall of storage cabinets that reach from floor to ceiling hold all the paraphenalia and allow the rest of the space in this designer's studio in Stockholm to remain clear and undisturbed by excess clutter. At each table is a modern classic chair design – one, the Wishbone by Hans Wegner, the other the 3117 designed by Arne Jacobsen.

MacGregor sense, does not really function effectively as a work space; without insulation and often erected straight onto the open ground, and so damp to boot, it can be as hot as it gets in summer and colder than you could ever wish in winter. The new garden offices – far closer to the raising of a summerhouse rather than of a potting shed – are usually pre-constructed and timber clad, and well-insulated, many with double glazing. So advanced is the industry that even quite modest models come prepared for immediate electricity installation – usually run in a cable from the main house. They have

Even the most basic of garden rooms – or in this case, perhaps, garden shed – can be made not only attractive, but positively inviting. The wooden floor has been stripped, the plank wall painted and a curtain hung at the window. A table of some vintage, a chair and a set of coat hooks on the wall make up the equipment, but with a strong table lamp, a radio, a knitting basket and a pile of books, what more could any one want.

OPPOSITE: Up beneath the eaves of the roof, a functional and spacious office has been created, combining practicality and imagination. A sturdy wooden table, an equally sturdy chair and a separate table for open-plan storage are combined with an elegant desk light and, for good measure, a striking candelabra.

wooden floors, can even come ready equipped
with shelves and desktop – and are a short
but definitive walk from the house. Designs
range hugely in price and style, from rustic,
verandah-clad nostalgia to the contemporary,
almost futuristic. And best of all – in most
cases, depending a bit on their dimensions –

planning permission is not required
(although, as usual, it is always best to check
with your local planning department first).

Wherever you finally decide to hang your
hat, a sense of separation from home life –
as much psychological as physical – is vital.
Equally as important in the new zone is

If you are making a small space, or part of a space into a working area, a lack of clutter and simplicity of surroundings is important. Here, that has been achieved by storing almost everything behind doors and keeping the colour scheme to monotones.

OPPOSITE: Even the most unpromising space can be converted into a serviceable and work-friendly office area; this office has been created in a mews house with very high ceilings as well as undivided floor space. To break up the space, mezzanine levels were created, one of which has been made into this office, the floor of which has been coated with resin and marble shingle, reminiscent of a beach house.

maintaining a sense of order. A private space should be satisfying to the soul and that only happens when there is order. For many of us this particular virtue does not come easily, but order isn't a luxury – it's a necessity, and any space that involves moving pieces of paper around needs some sort of tidiness routine. The more order there is, the more compact the space you will be able to operate from. First thing is to ascertain just what pieces of paper, loose files, and so on you will have around you, and after that, simple as it sounds, is to decide exactly where you need to keep these things – i.e. not just somewhere in that space, but exactly where, based on the need-to-know principle; information that

Almost any space inside or outside the home can be turned into a functional and attractive office

you need on a daily basis, close by; other stuff – necessary but less often – further away (but easily identified). Tidy areas stay tidy, messy areas grow: we are all inclined to chuck more stuff on to a pile that already has junk there – it seems the obvious thing to do, but the higher the pile, the more difficult it becomes to bring it down to size.

In a rustic country house, a friendly home office has been created. The ideal area in which to work in perfect peace, every inch of available space has been utilized with bookcases that run to the ceiling with, below them, deep cupboards and drawers, all of which leaves just about enough room for a desk, side table and chair.

HOME-OFFICE CONSIDERATIONS

* If you run a business from home and you intend to hold meetings in your office, it is psychologically important to position your desk to face the door, rather than a wall.

* Analyse your own storage needs before setting up the office, making sure that you have a place for everything you need around you.

* There is no need, in your own private space, for a colour scheme based on all the myriad shades of muted magnolia. Think about which colours you personally respond to: both stimulating and peaceful.

* Fluorescent ceiling lighting has no place in a home office; instead light the space with a considered combination of specific task lighting and softer ambient lighting.

* Take time to look for the right desk lamp that not only works for your particular set-up but that is good looking also.

* Ensure you have enough electric sockets for every piece of essential and necessary equipment. Nothing is more frustrating than constantly swapping plugs.

* A telephone is a necessity when you work at home – make sure you have a telephone socket or cordless phone to hand. Likewise, if you require the internet, ensure you have a socket or are within range of the wi-fi box.

In a most minimal house, a working room has been created that takes advantage of the ample natural light. The furniture is carefully considered – the desk is from a Swedish castle, the chair was found at auction, and the table light is a classic 1950s' design by Arne Jacobsen.

OPPOSITE: A place for peaceful contemplation and time to think. These are the benefits of a private place of one's own; a place where there is no need for expensive fixtures and fittings, just painted floor boards and white-painted walls.

Once you have your new super-space, you must think how, and with what equipment, you need to furnish it. Arts and crafts usually have their specific needs and physical positions; designing an office space is often slightly more difficult. Perhaps the first essential is not to reproduce other offices and other office conditions that you have known. This is your space and the corporate view is unimportant. Although the computer, printer, fax and so on, are an important part of a smooth running office, there is often no need for them to hold centre stage, if you prefer to keep them on shelves or behind doors. Every office needs basic supplies – usually stationery based – but rather in the same way that writing a list of larder

In a perfect home office, a sense of separation from daily domestic life is vital

essentials is always more notable for its omissions than its additions, so setting down a list of home office requirements will never really hit the spot; one size does certainly not fit all. Even as I write, new products are being designed, produced and sold to make your life even easier and more productive than ever, and it is not difficult to find, through catalogues and specialist suppliers, what is new, good and almost made for you.

A dual-purpose room that really works – part spare bedroom with a pull-out sofabed, and also a home office, complete with a comprehensive system of drawers and built-in shelves so that everything has its own place.

SHARED SPACES

If you are working from home and there is not the space for a dedicated room in which you can work then, at the very least, try to find the best space possible where you are least likely to be interrupted and where concentration can be given to the task in hand, as in these circumstances it is even more important that both office and home life can be separated when the need arises. Think psychologically, and realize that the most important thing about occupying shared space for your own work, that is to say sharing a space with others – usually your

ABOVE: In the corner of a busy room, a desk abuts onto a room divider that offers storage behind sliding doors, thus making the whole area remarkably self-contained.

LEFT: This chic London flat is an exemplar of the idea of a multi-functioning space, combining as it does a smart living area with a small but efficient work area at one end, that is designed in the same sophisticated style as the rest of the room. One section of the window is made up of opaque glass bricks, which give privacy and diffuse the light. Behind a sofa, a desk and chair are tucked neatly away.

family – is for both you, and them, to think of it as your own in the same way that you would think of an entire room of your own. For, in everything except walls and doors, it is your own, no matter how small or awkward the space, and it is important that everyone around you realizes that.

If you are going to set up your office or work space in part of the family living room, so that your desk or work table becomes part of the larger, communal room, the desk top itself must be recognized as sacrosanct – for your things alone, and under no circumstances

ABOVE LEFT: At the end of a corridor, a small space has been made into a narrow, but well-conceived working area with room for on one side, tall book shelves, and on the other a long two-seater desk.

ABOVE RIGHT: Neatly fitted into a small space in a passage, this scaled down desk offers a work base where belongings can be parked, and necessities stored for safe keeping.

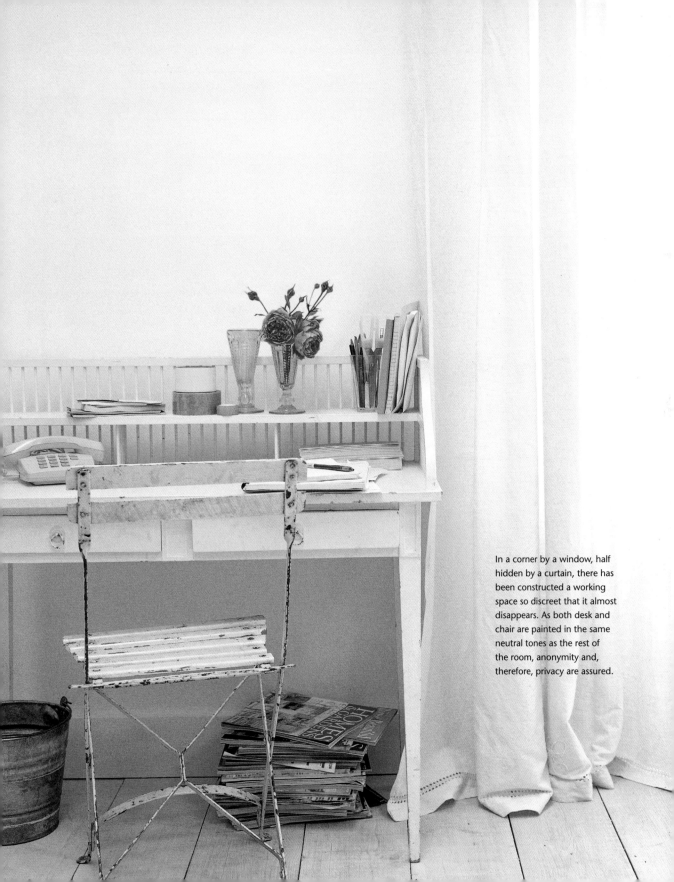

In a corner by a window, half hidden by a curtain, there has been constructed a working space so discreet that it almost disappears. As both desk and chair are painted in the same neutral tones as the rest of the room, anonymity and, therefore, privacy are assured.

In another dead space,
between two windows, a desk
and an Arne Jacobsen 'Grand
Prix' chair have been turned
into a vibrant, intricate,
decorative composition, with
a colourful display of African
textiles, masks and artefacts.

a depository for other people's cups, books or newspapers. If you are able, try to position the desk, and the associated furniture, in front of a window. As well as giving you valuable daylight, the frame that the window makes around the desk area has the visual effect of delineating the space, of separating it, even if there are other activities going on in the rest of the room.

Outward appearances will make an immediate difference and mark your turf visually. If there is no architectural break between the two areas, then you might want to half-blend into the rest of the room

ABOVE LEFT: This otherwise dead space, beside the fireplace and under the window, is too small for conventional furniture but perfect for a small writing desk and elegant painted bamboo chair.

ABOVE RIGHT: What might otherwise be construed as a large walk-in cupboard with a window could also be seen as a very small, but fit for purpose, working area.

using the same style and colours, to avoid a jarring contrast between differing styles of decoration. Choose a style that, even if not entirely the same, will work with the overall scheme, and try to look for furniture that will work in the larger context – a desk perhaps that is also part table, or else a decorative piece in its own right.

On the other hand, if the room is large enough (do not try to divide a small room – it will simply end up looking like two cramped, uncomfortable little rooms) you might like to physically demarcate the area with a room divider of some sort. If you are lucky enough to live in a large, light loft or warehouse space, a structural option which can give architectural interest as well as partial privacy is to have built, surrounding the study area, a short wall at right angles to a structural wall, forming an L, which hides the work space, whilst providing room for a good-sized desk space as well as shelving and

In a converted loft in Manhattan, a partition half-wall has been built so that a working area with privacy can be created behind it. Within this area is multi-purpose shelving for storage, as well as a desk that runs the full length of the wall.

storage on the inner face of the L. The outer face of the L wall, meanwhile, can be treated decoratively as part of the larger room, with pictures and furniture against it.

If such a structure seems too permanent, there are other design solutions which start with the simplest one of all – a panelled screen which is relatively light-weight, adaptable and usually decorative, and acts as a psychological as well as a decorative barrier. There are so many styles of folding screens, ranging from the antique to the contemporary, that any decorative style can usually be accommodated. They are even easily made from panels of

To ensure privacy, a room that is shared will need some sort of room divider

plywood that can then be painted, papered or fabric-covered according to your own taste.

Slightly less mobile, a free-standing bookcase with a solid back could form a partition wall, positioned so that the books can either face into the wider world or be your own shelving and storage system. If there is sufficient room, a pair of free-standing bookcases, arranged back to back, work even better. Even a seating arrangement – a sofa or two chairs – although not ideal, would at least suggest a psychological barrier, if not a physical one.

If the room that you are dividing is a bedroom, a simple divider, and one that would not seem out of place, would be a heavy curtain hung from ceiling-suspended tracks or rail; furnishing fabric, perhaps a pattern that worked with the curtains or bed, but also tapestries, shawls, or even bright blankets could conceal the office space.

If you cannot, or would rather not, be part of living room or bedroom life, then you must find somewhere else in the house that will give you both privacy and room for your things. The best way to do this is to try to look at every bit of your home in a slightly different way. In a building with which we are familiar, we habitually follow the same paths, both noticing and ignoring the same things every day. We walk past alcoves, skirt half-landings, and simply don't see odd angled spaces under the stairs. And as for cupboards – many of us would be hard-pressed to list, without thinking, how many and where the cupboards are.

OPPOSITE: Heavy curtains along one end of a bedroom hide a wall of storage and a desktop where a small working area, complete with everything that is needed, can be easily contained – and disguised when the room is being used for relaxation.

RIGHT, ABOVE AND BELOW: A clever wooden concertina folding screen, purposely designed for the space, closes off a comfortable working area from the rest of the room; windows with wide vertical blinds make the space even more self contained.

So walk round your home when it is silent – preferably when it is empty and all the other occupants are otherwise engaged. What has possibilities? Against which of the windows can you envisage a desk? In which corner can you see your possessions stowed? And in which dark, hidden-away place could a small hive of techno-industry be set up? At the same time, think about what you – in a perfect world – would like to have in your space; a view? Or at any rate, natural light? Or somewhere where excess noise is muffled?

Start first with any possible corners – so often overlooked in the planning of a home office. Too small and inconvenient to hold a large piece of furniture, a corner with judiciously chosen furniture and equipment can make the best home office – neat and functional without intruding into the use and space of the larger room. A desk placed into the right angle, preferably with drawers, and in the angle itself, free-standing pieces of furniture like small filing cabinets or plan chests, with shelves above that fit into the corner or run around it, mean that neatness and order can be easily achieved. And if all this sounds too immovable, the hard-working

A small working area that bears the unmistakable imprint of its owner, scattered as it is with objects that have a particularly personal presence. A wall-fixed adjustable lamp frees up some useful desk space.

OPPOSITE, ABOVE AND BELOW: In a studio flat, a clever space has been made for work within the sitting area. A waist-height shelf runs the length of one wall. Between the fireplace and the window the shelf becomes deeper, forming an office area with desktop, comfortable chair and task lighting.

case study

Period houses – particularly those of the 18th and early 19th century – were built to ideal, classical proportions and often furnished with great simplicity of line with just a few well-chosen pieces of furniture in each room and deep cupboards built into the walls to house the paraphernalia of everyday life.

Architect William Smalley has taken advantage of this fact in his flat on the upper floors of an elegant 18th century house in Soho. In this perfectly proportioned room, behind panelled walls of great beauty, the pair of original cupboards on either side of the elegant fireplace have been converted into an office storage system of functional efficiency. On one side is what might be termed a media-computer centre with all things electrical as well as storage for boxes and files. On the other side of the fireplace is his cupboard-reference library with books and magazines stored on deep shelves that extend to ceiling height. Against the cool neutral colours of the room, the insides of the two cupboards have been painted in contrasting shades which are not too bright and not too warm – a very 18th century touch.

RIGHT: On either side of the fireplace in this panelled sitting room are cupboards that have been made into integral elements of a home office. One side is filled with the working components, and the other, window, side is a home for reference books and magazines.

Typically, houses of this period – the 18th century – were often built with deep, roomy cupboards. This example, behind an original door, has been fitted out with sturdy, deep shelves, and now houses a mini office and bulky storage system, complete with computer, modem, sound system and even box files.

A sliding door conceals this cupboard-cum-office from the wider world beyond. Large enough for a desk and chair, when closed there is no intimation that a private space lies on the other side.

OPPOSITE: As pretty as a picture, this period desk is quite at home in the equally pretty period drawing room. The arrangement of miniature pictures above the desk is a charming decorative detail.

corner could even house a portable office: a mobile computer station, and a trolley with shelves to act as filing and storage.

Then there is the office-in-a-cupboard. In many ways, a deep cupboard is the perfect module for a shut-away office, a fact which many companies have recognized and there are now several interesting design options on the market for systems that can convert what seems a normal cupboard into something which, when opened, might include a slide-out work surface, complete with trays for computer, and integral filing and storage cabinets. On any remaining wall surface inside the cupboard hang narrow shelving,

Almost no area is too small to make into an attractive and organized work space

and equip the inside of the cupboard door with a pinboard, and then all that is needed is a chair (which can be conveniently kept outside the cupboard door).

A corridor is another space that may not immediately suggest itself as an office but that, with a little bit of planning, can be

surprisingly effective. There may be room to fit a desk-height shelf along the wall, even one that is hinged to sit flush to the wall when not in use. Above, there could be open shelves, or – sometimes better in an enclosed space – closed cupboards to hide the files and office paraphernalia.

OPPOSITE: At the top of a flight of stairs, there is enough room in an otherwise unusable space to fit in a desk, chair and lamp, with a single storage chest at one side.

ABOVE LEFT: In a narrow hallway leading towards a spiral staircase, an office space has been created behind cabinet doors, using space which would have otherwise been redundant.

ABOVE RIGHT: A small-scale table against a low wall with, beside it, a wall-hung set of bookshelves makes a study space which is completely in proportion.

If your house is old and with lots of stairs, there may be space at the top of a flight where a desktop or even a small free-standing desk can be placed, with perhaps a small bookshelf along the wall, or a wall-hung set of shelves. This is the spot to use a desk that was made to be admired as well as to be used.

Perhaps there is a half-landing available, which can, in many ways, be a perfect work space: part of the house but architecturally defined as a separate place. I was once lucky enough to live in a house which had a half-landing with a window looking out over the neighbouring gardens. The space was tiny, but large enough for a chair and a desk pushed against the window with a pair of wall-hung shelves on either side. It was a wonderful place to sit and work – and to look out at the gardens, obviously.

LEFT: Definitely part of a larger room, indeed not immediately identifiable as a private working space, this elegant bureau, framed by two striking chairs is given away only by the work light on the top.

BELOW: The space beneath the staircase can often be utilized for a desk or work space. Ensure that the chosen desk is of the right dimensions for the available space.

OPPOSITE: Beneath the eaves, the residual angled space has been turned into a clever purpose-built office space where natural light floods the working area.

The most basic – and almost universally ignored – space in many houses is that found under the stairs. It may be a junk cupboard that follows the angle of the staircase, or it may be just an awkward open space. But regardless, it can often be used, depending on its height and depth, either as a complete office space, or at the very least, as storage space for a desk set elsewhere in the room.

Lastly, if you really cannot find any space large enough to convert into somewhere that you can both work and store what you need, at least find a place where all your files and equipment can be stored safely together without danger of them being 'tidied' away.

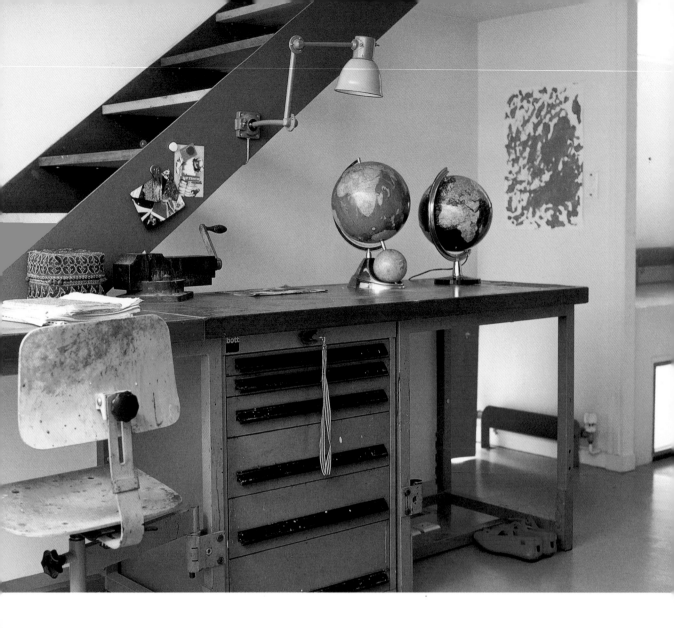

The otherwise difficult place beneath the stairs can often be used to create an attractive working area

One of the most difficult aspects of working from home is continually having to move papers from one place to another. If you at least have a dedicated tidy storage space that is separate from your desk and computer, that side of life will become a little easier.

OPPOSITE: A working space that succeeds on every level. The staircase structure itself is used as a base from which to anchor the adjustable sturdy work lamp, whilst a desk tucks neatly into the angle of the wall.

ABOVE: Within a contemporary dining room, an unobtrusive cupboard front opens to reveal a perfect working space, complete with comprehensive pull-out work station.

RIGHT: A cupboard office complete with shelves and a desk top has been cleverly built into the sharp angle of the stairs, making maximum use of the awkward space.

In this designer's studio, there is no need for extra display, the designer's work providing adequate adornment. The furnishings and equipment are simple: a large window for essential daylight, a long trestle table with enough room to manoeuvre, and a wide chest with shallow drawers to hold paper of different sizes.

SEWING, CRAFT & ARTISTS' ROOMS

One of the greatest luxuries – a greater luxury even, I think, than having a study heaving with tempting, luscious books – is to have a dedicated room or space where you can be creative – oh the joy of it – spending your time in jewellery-making, potting, painting or drawing, sewing or knitting, in a place that is your own with all your tools, work and inspiration around you.

Although many people enjoy the pleasure of creating for its own sake, many others create as a professional business; whichever route you have chosen, the one thing that is essential to both scenarios is a well-organized space – and doubly so if this space is part of a room that also has another function.

If your creative aspirations are veering in a home business direction, there will also have to be space somewhere for the actual business side of the enterprise – a place for the keeping and filing of records, and all the other elements of an efficient work place – even if it is as simple a solution as a pair of miniature filing cabinets or paper drawers that sit beneath the work table.

ABOVE LEFT: Jam jars with an assortment of tops, many of which you can create yourself, are the perfect recycled containers for small pieces of equipment, from silk thread to brass tacks.

ABOVE RIGHT: A sense of harmony is apparent in the use of the same shape of container in a variety of sizes for different materials: here brushes are kept in white china pots, and paints in cheap round boxes, that are stacked one upon the other.

After these perhaps boring, but essential aspects have been dealt with, the next task is to identify what equipment, tools and material you will need and where everything – large or small, but particularly large – will be stored. More than in any other room, this is a space where there really must be a place for everything and everything in its place. Large necessities such as a sewing machine,

This old barn in Normandy, which has been converted into an artist's studio, has the great luxury of having enough storage for all materials and equipment, plus bags of natural light and floor space a plenty for easels and work surfaces.

An artist's studio is somewhere where there really must be a place for everything and everything in its place

dressmaker's dummy, drawing table, potting wheel, or easel, for example, will usually need a lot of space, so think about how best they will fit within your preferred floor plan. You may also need large-scale open storage – perhaps free-standing metal warehouse shelving or adjustable wooden shelves or racks for un-fired pottery, bolts of fabric or large canvases.

Think also about the smaller items, the wherewithals for your particular art – the paints and brushes, the needles and threads, the skeins of yarn: how will you best store them in order to be able to access them easily? Perhaps you would like these in open

OPPOSITE: Is this for display or function? A bit of both, with a fine antique side table arranged with some of the tools of the artist's trade, ranging from a pigment-grinding pestle and mortar to wooden clamps to pots of brushes and a well-worn pair of boots.

ABOVE AND RIGHT: A spacious working space is made by erecting a simple pergola-like trellis which is floored with rough wooden boards and then covered with clear, rain resistant panes.

LEFT AND FAR LEFT:
A communal studio, where more than one artist is working, must be arranged in a way that gives everyone enough creative space around them. Organized storage is the key to communal life, and here this is provided with a recycled set of filing cabinets that run the length of the wall, where deep drawers can hold everything in labelled and sectioned compartments, leaving the table clear. The room is lit by low-hung ceiling lamps that straddle the length of the communal work table. An assortment of work chairs, each of them adjustable, are set on either side.

storage, where they can be easily seen, or you may prefer them behind closed doors. There is a wide range of relatively inexpensive storage options available, particularly for small pieces of equipment, limited only by the breadth of your imagination. The right free-standing cupboard, for example, can become an almost self-contained storage unit, and offers an opportunity for a bit of positive reclamation. Suites of bedroom furniture – matching wardrobes, chests and beds – are no longer fashionable and many a serviceable old wardrobe can be found languishing in a second-hand shop or at a house clearance sale. It may

LEFT, ABOVE AND BELOW: Up in the air, at the top of a building, and with an outside terrace beyond, is a space just made to be a studio, with enough room to display works, a plethora of good quality daylight and an adjustable, tilting table – this is every artist's dream.

OPPOSITE: Everything is purely functional in this studio – the most basic of metal shelving, and equally basic table, plus a chair that must have started life in an industrial environment – and it all works really well.

Using what is readily to hand is a good way to furnish a creative space

at first appear ugly, but with a coat or two of paint, such a piece, particularly one with double doors, can swiftly be transformed into a veritable creative centre. Shelves installed within the body of the cupboard and the insides of the doors fitted out to hold small items could work for anything from painting equipment, to needle and wool work.

A basic chest of drawers, too, can be brought into creative service, easily converted into a complete storage system with light-weight plywood divisions – like those in a cutlery holder – or even ready-made cutlery trays slotted into each drawer so that everything from a scissors collection to tins of pins,

case study

Emily Chalmers is a stylist, author and owner of the successful quirky interiors shop, Caravan, in Shoreditch, east London. Her former home, a converted warehouse in Shoreditch, is a testament to her originality in finding ways to make working at home and domestic life compatible.

Like all good stylists, Emily is always sensitive to the beauty of objects, pattern and design, and her home is living witness to that – everywhere are hanging lengths of fabric, feathers, all things pretty and baubles and beads. Why hide things that you like? Why indeed, asks Emily: 'I love vintage floral prints and have lots of patterned clothes I hang on the wall. It makes more sense than hiding them in the wardrobe – and also makes the space cosy and warm.' Her desk, which sits below some shelves that are as decoratively arranged as the rest of the space, is divided from the larger space by an unusual curtain – more than a dozen vintage scarves tacked together to form a hanging of great originality. On the other side of the scarf-curtain is an old metal postal cabinet which acts as a storage unit for Emily's collection of vintage textiles. Cheap? Yes. Cheerful? Definitely. Successful? Resoundingly.

FAR LEFT: Dividing the desk area from the rest of the living space is a curtain made of twelve vintage scarves, loosely sewn together. A perfect example of function merging into display.

LEFT: The wall above the desk is used as a perpetual inspiration board, with shelves holding all things decorative as well as some things useful.

OPPOSITE: On the other side of the scarf-curtain is an old metal post-office cabinet, whose pigeonholes were originally used for letters, but are now home to a collection of vintage textiles.

The one thing that is not essential when setting up your own studio is buckets of cash, as is well demonstrated by this working studio. A screen made of shutters closes the space off, and the furniture consists of very cheap and very cheerful pieces.

OPPOSITE: Simple is as simple does: in this all-wood cabin, a basic trestle table is put up beneath a window, in between a pair of matching metal trollies. A collection of antique blue glass decorates the shelf below the eaves.

tape-measures, thread, paint brushes, pens and inks can be kept in order. And around the room, make more storage space for small, loose items by requisitioning useful pieces from elsewhere in the house: a mug stand, a coat rack with pegs or hooks to hang things on; a peg or cork board to secure important pieces of paper, and to keep safe things, like different coloured embroidery threads, which might otherwise inexplicably disappear. Tool and fishing tackle boxes, portable knife drawers and glass storage jars also make great storage solutions.

Of course, assessing what equipment you will need and where it should be stored leads to thoughts about the organizational aspect of your space. The creative process – whether

Ensure that there are enough surfaces around you to keep all essentials close to hand

it is painting at an easel, sewing at a machine or by hand, or potting at a wheel – consists of a series of procedures which have to be carried out in a specific order. Of course you know how you like to work, but before you lay out your perfect studio, it often helps if you verbally identify your particular routine, noting your path between the different points of work, and whether you could work in a more efficient or labour-saving way. It's really back to ergonomics and the golden triangle again – although in the case of arts

CREATIVE STORAGE IDEAS FOR BITS AND PIECES

* Traditional bulb-shaped glass preserving jars with hinged lids are great for attractively storing everything from cotton reels to buttons. Use different sizes mixed together.

* Pinboards and padded boards criss-crossed with contrasting ribbon (mix different colours) are good for notes and aide-memoires as well as inspirational pictures and bits.

* Old printers' trays – shallow, wooden boxes divided into many compartments – can be hung vertically on the wall, the compartments used for everything from coloured inks to boxes of paperclips.

* Tool boards – the sort you find in a garage – can be used to hang larger pieces of craft equipment such as scissors and shears.

* Hang reels of ribbon on a narrow brass rail or an expanding wire – the sort used for café curtains.

* Often found, cheaply at auction, are old trunks, sometimes with faded, exotic labels – perfect for storing lengths of material and folio size papers.

* And if you are lucky enough to find a vertical wardrobe (cabin) trunk, your creative storage problem is solved in one perfect swoop!

* Use book shelves creatively – mix groups of books with decorative flat-bottomed baskets holding papers and files.

* As well as being easily accessible, pens and pencils look positively fetching in old jugs/pitchers and decorative mugs.

* Do not despise the conventional, portable cutlery unit for storing fiddly things close to hand.

RIGHT: Creative storage starts with creative cupboards: here an old wooden cupboard that may once have been used to store food, has had the original chicken wire in the panels replaced with panels made from old striped linen towels.

ABOVE LEFT: A cheap and cheerful, as well as very attractive, way to hide the storage that sits beneath a worktop is to make a curtain that runs the length of the lower shelves.

ABOVE RIGHT: In an otherwise functional area, the work space of a perfumier, the tools of her trade, the bottles and jars ranged in neat rows in shelves above the desk, are both functional and decorative.

and crafts, you may well have more than three essential sites that you work between. Think also about what sort of shape you like to work in: some prefer a slightly rounded U-shape, others a galley, or an L-shaped space. This is a question of your personal preference, what you are working with, and, to a large extent, habit.

Patently some crafts – jewellery-making and pottery spring immediately to mind – cannot be undertaken in a room, such as the kitchen or living room, where there is a lot of busy, all-day traffic. Not only is the process of creating in these instances complex, and

Nothing could be simpler than this work space, furnished as it is with the most basic and functional of equipment, but all arranged with a sense of order that makes the whole space harmonious. An existing alcove has been turned into deep book shelves where large files are kept, as well as a small filing chest. Rolls of material are stacked in the corner, and a single painting on the wall provides the only considered decorative touch.

A professional artist's space – a studio where inspiration must come naturally, blessed as it is with enough space for several easels, as well as moveable storage in the form of lightweight tables. Light is distributed evenly, coming from above and from long, narrow windows at floor level.

OPPOSITE ABOVE: Draughtsmanship requires very precise lighting as well as enough space to have all instruments to hand. Ample natural light is augmented by two adjustable task lights.

OPPOSITE BELOW: Used both for homework and crafts, this work space has been carved out of a corner and furnished both simply and economically with recycled school desks and a blackboard.

often delicate, but half-finished pieces often cannot
be easily moved until they are completed, and the
equipment required for such crafts – worktops and
benches as well as a plethora of heavy stuff, and
fine-tuned precision tools – usually needs permanent,
fixed space. If there is no whole room available in
your home, it is sometimes possible to occupy part
of a spare bedroom, or even a semi-redundant
dining-room, as long as thought is given as to allow
the room to continue to work in its alternative mode:

As long as you create enough space to easily store some of the often bulky materials associated with needlework, the basic equipment that is required is usually minimal – like here, where a sturdy worktop, made from reclaimed boarding, is set onto an equally sturdy industrial metal base.

OPPOSITE: In this sewing room, the machine sits neatly at the back of a wooden working table. It would be hard not to be inspired by the creative board above, studded as it is with paper images and notes, miniature artefacts and pieces that are simply pretty.

something as straightforward as an old door on a pair of trestles. And somewhere to sit – a comfortable swivel chair is good if you have a smooth floor surface over which you can whizz from one zone to another.

The right choice of flooring is important, if not vital. This is not the place for deep pile rugs, or even fitted carpet. Activities that involve working with materials from clay to paints, or even thread and pins, require a floor surface that can be easily cleaned – and kept clean – and which does not act as a bunker in which pins (usually sharp end up)

Make sure your flooring is fit for purpose – paints, clay and pins are not compatible with deep pile carpets!

sometimes something as simple as a room divider such as a heavy, bright linen or canvas curtain on a ceiling-hung pole, or a screen, decorative in itself, provides a solution.

As well as specialist equipment, some basic pieces of furniture will probably be required, depending, of course, on what sort of work you are going to do. Everyone needs some sort of table or desktop – as specialized, perhaps, as a draughtsman's tilting table, or

and other potential hazards can lurk. Wood and tiles are both options, but top of the poll for many comes linoleum – a warm, natural material, available in rolls as well as tiles, which means that the floor space can be covered without too many seams, and is therefore easy to keep clean.

If you have natural lighting, particularly – if you are painting – natural northern light, then you have an inbuilt advantage. But if

Even though this particular arrangement of space might, at first sight, seem slightly random, in fact everything has its place and is conveniently, and rather efficiently to hand, with each fabric sample on the board above the work table, having been embroidered with its provenance.

OPPOSITE: A simple, effective sewing space with a table large enough to hold a sewing machine, a basic chair fitted with a pretty slip cover, and a large window giving ample natural light.

OPPOSITE: In part of a sewing area, full advantage is made of one of the walls, using it as the ideal place to keep everything from samples of textiles to inspirational pictures and drawings. A moveable dressmaker's dummy and equipment trolley give the space added flexibility.

RIGHT: Deep and wide shelves built into an existing alcove mean that bulky and fiddly items, kept in containers that range from a hatbox to a wrought iron jardinière, can be stored above floor level. A pinboard serves as a work-in-progress board, with constant updates on the project.

the only available space in your home is in a dark basement, then better by far to use it and plan your artificial lighting to reproduce natural light – something which is far easier today with the development of lighting that is as close as possible to daylight. Augment this

Always store any materials where they can be easily seen and are close to hand

with very specific, flexible task lighting.

Ventilation is important in any craft room, particularly if you are working with firing devices or electrical equipment. If there is no natural ventilation in the form of a window, look into installing some sort of extractor fan system.

Another essential emphasized by all dedicated craftspeople is a source of water within the room, and it is true that, save for needlework and wool work, a basin or sink

is an enormous advantage. But if there is no source and it is too expensive to install, then I think that a waterless space of your own is still infinitely better than no space at all!

And once you have allowed for all these practical parts of the perfect creative space, do not forget the most valuable element of all – peace and tranquillity. It may not be entirely possible, but on the other hand it may be as simple as a nice heavy door that can be quietly, but firmly closed.

SPACES FOR CHILDREN & TEENS

ABOVE: Into quite a small area are arranged and contained all the right elements for a space in which to work, study and just be. A large enough desk space with a comfortable chair, maximum storage of a fairly basic nature, a sound system and room for a collection of guitars and amplifiers.

OPPOSITE: Far from childish, this is a work room that is sophisticated and grown up, whilst still acknowledging the pleasure of childhood, as in the group of old friends displayed on the shelf above the well-arranged work space.

Perhaps one of the most important things that you can give any child, – and in particular, an older child – is a personal space within the home that they can feel is totally theirs, to use as they will (within reason!) and, importantly, that can be decorated in a way that will please them and, even better, inspire them. Just as for an adult, a child or teenager, no matter how noisy or hectic their life might seem to those older than them, also needs a place of order in their lives.

A child's – and teenager's – life is filled with have-tos: have to finish homework; have to complete this or that; have to be in bed, have tea, lunch and so on. A space of their own must, therefore, be

able to provide them with the freedom and the space to do all the things they want to do; to relax, study and store their possessions – finding space for toys and books, paper and paints, CDs and DVDs, sound systems and computers. So, when thinking about the design of a child or teenage bedroom, storage – what kind, how much – is an extremely important element. There is just so much stuff – in the form of toys when children are younger, and just plain stuff when they are older. (And that is without the

ABOVE AND RIGHT: Storage is of course an important element of the well-planned children's bedroom, and it should be storage that is accessible to the occupant of the room; clothes that can be hung on hooks that are low enough, crayons and pencils close to a work table, and books and a petite desk and chair ready at the right level for the reader.

OPPOSITE: A place where more than one can study and play at the same time. The edges of the room are fitted with tables and chairs, whilst possessions and tools are arranged in every other available space.

case study

There is, in Battersea, a large rambling Victorian school with high ceilings and tall windows, which has been converted over the last few years into some of the most imaginative apartments in London.

In one of them, Michaelis Boyd, the architectural practice whose watchwords are 'space', 'flow' and 'light', have created an apartment which holds a teenage heaven and haven – a separate area innovatively designed where three siblings can work, rest and play in style. The high ceilinged space has been utilized to create a mezzanine level on which – rather than separate bedrooms – are three sleeping platforms, divided from each other by low, partition walls. Below the mezzanine

sleeping platforms there is a shared space of areas intended for homework and study, with large desk surfaces and ample book shelves. Communication portholes between the study areas mean that whilst there is a sense of peace there is also company, and equally importantly, the space is peppered with quiet places to sit and read or just be peaceful. White walls prevail with a few carefully chosen pictures and photographs.

This is a shared working space and is equipped to be as professional and efficient as possible. A single flowing work desk surface has individual task lighting spaced along its length, and ample space for books on shelves above.

OPPOSITE ABOVE: Up on the mezzanine floor, instead of bedrooms, are separate sleeping platforms for all three siblings, separated one from the other by low, curved partition walls.

OPPOSITE BELOW: The easiest way to get from the sleeping platforms down to the study and relaxation areas on the lower level is – obviously – by pole. What could be simpler?

OPPOSITE: Colour is a great unifier in a room in which there is a lot going on, and the strong blue fireplace wall brings together the bookcases, storage units, trolleys and desk in a clever and coherent way.

RIGHT: Not much extra decoration is needed in the average working room. Here, in a room based around work and music, a single strong image on the wall is all that is required to add a personal element, and bring in a touch of fun to this teenager's space.

shoes, the clothes, the sports equipment.) The storage systems that seem to work best are adaptable, which often means modular, and furniture pieces can also be augmented with flexible containers. Everything from baskets to boxes on wheels can be brought into play – anything as long as the contents can be identified quickly and easily.

Beds can provide storage solutions too: many come with with storage drawers below, and a gallery bed can become an entire unit

The storage systems that seem to work best are those which can easily adapt to new interests

with a big-enough desk and shelving below.

Every child – young or old – needs a desk, or better still a work space in their room. If it's not homework, it's art, model-making or computers, all of which need a large flat surface with open shelving above, if possible,

and storage below, if possible. Shelving should be as adjustable as the space allows so it can adapt to changing interests as well as grow with the growing child; if they can't reach it, they won't use it – and they certainly won't put it away.

Lighting should be as flexible as the rest of the room's furnishings: think of using reading lights and task lights near the bed and work areas, but in the rest of the room, using some ambient lighting that will provide a relaxing and peaceful atmosphere.

The criteria for a work surface should probably rest more on the indestructible than high-design, although there is no reason why the two may not be combined. In a smaller room, a drop-leg table attached to the wall will serve the purpose well.

Free-standing computer workstations are a useful addition to a teenage bedroom: often on castors and brightly coloured, the space is designed to hold monitor, modem and other necessaries, thus freeing up other space.

ABOVE LEFT AND RIGHT: A good and adaptable working space has been practically carved out of the rafters in this attic space; a long, continuous desktop runs along one wall, and above it brackets have been affixed to the beams to create an equally long storage shelf.

OPPOSITE: The smallest corner of a room can become a more than adequate work space with a bit of creative thinking. Here, a built-in desk and a shelving unit divided into compartments of varying sizes fits the bill perfectly.

OPPOSITE: Simple beyond anything, this is, nonetheless a perfect working space, with the wall behind the desktop used as an inspirational explosion of both colour and creative ideas.

ABOVE LEFT: A clever use of the alcove on one side of a chimney breast, turned into a shelving unit with the base extended across to become a desktop.

ABOVE RIGHT: A decorative table abuts shelves that run across the wall behind, and which act as a catch-all open storage unit.

The best floor covering is one that repels knocked-over this and ground-in that. It's no fun on either side when spilt liquids and food become an issue. Better to have sealed wood, linoleum or some other wipe-free surface, covered with large washable rugs.

Finally, teenagers (and younger children too) like privacy and adults dislike noise. In their rooms, ambient noise – television, music, and so on – is a given, so it is no bad idea when thinking about the design of teenage rooms to make sure that the room has some sort of unobtrusive sound proofing in the form of, perhaps, heavy curtains as well as a solid door – privacy for them, and peace in our time.

In a converted loft space, one wall has been imaginatively converted into three semi-detached studies, where privacy and peace but also companionship at a distance are assured. Each has been individually decorated to the taste of its occupant and industrial metal ladders rise from each pod to a platform bed above.

INDEX

Figures in italics indicate captions.

ARCHITECTS, ARTISTS, DESIGNERS AND BUSINESS OWNERS

WHOSE WORK HAS BEEN FEATURED IN THIS BOOK:

A.L.M. INTERIOR DESIGN
Andy L. Marcus
935 Westbourne Drive, # 201
West Hollywood, CA 90069
alminteriordesign@earthlink.net
+1 213 716 9797
Page 1

ANDREW HAIR
Tapis Vert
+44 (0)20 8678 1408
tapis.vert@virgin.net
Page 161

ANK VD PLUIJM
www.householdhardware.nl
Page 146

ANN SHORE
Creative
Story
The Old Truman Brewery
4–5 Dray Walk, off Brick Lane
London E1 6QL
+44 (0)20 7247 3137
Page 24

ANNABEL GREY
+44 (0)7860 500356
www.annabelgrey.com
annabel.grey@btinternet.com
Page 30

ANTHROPOLOGIE
www.anthropologie.com
Pages 43l, 74ar, 135

ASFOUR GUZY
www.asfourguzy.com
Pages 40, 41

ATLANTA BARTLETT
www.atlantabartlett.com
*Endpapers, pages 5b, 21al, 33, 55l,
61, 66, 69, 96, 107, 148*

BABYLON DESIGN LTD
now trades as Birgit Israel Home
www.birgitisrael.com
Pages 64, 65

BAILEYS
Whitecross Farm
Bridstow
Ross-on-Wye
Herefordshire HR9 6JU
www.baileyshome.com
Pages 5a, 36, 37, 42l, 139

BEACH STUDIOS
www.beachstudios.co.uk
*Endpapers, pages 5b, 21al, 33, 55l,
61, 66, 69, 96, 107, 148*

BELMONT FREEMAN ARCHITECTS
110 West 40th Street
New York, NY 10018
+1 212 382 3311
www.belmontfreeman.com
Page 32

BEN JOHNS CEO
Scout Ltd
(Bags and floor coverings)
1055 Thomas Jefferson Street NW
Washington DC 20007
+1 202 944 9590
ben@bungalowco.com
Pages 5ac, 152, 154

CARLA SAIBENE
Womenswear Collection,
Accessories and Antiques
Via San Maurilio 20
Milano
+39 2 77 33 15 70
xaibsrl@yahoo.com
Page 19 both

CASE FURNITURE LTD
189 Stonhouse Street
London SW4 6BB
+44 (0)20 7622 3506
www.casefurniture.co.uk
Pages 14, 34 both

CAVE INTERIORS
www.caveinteriors.com
Page 49br

CECILIA PROSERPIO
cecilia.proserpio@fastwebnet.it
Pages 22–23

CENTURY DESIGN
68 Marylebone High Street
London W1M 3AQ
modern@centuryd.com
www.centuryd.com
Page 118

CHRISTINA WILSON
www.christinawilson.co.uk
Page 93

**CLAESSON KOIVISTO RUNE
ARKITEKTKONTOR**
www.ckr.se
Page 102

COMMA
David Khouri
Architecture, Interiors & Furniture
149 Wooster Street, Suite 4NW
New York, NY 10012
+1 212 420 7866
www.comma-nyc.com
info@comma-nyc.com
Page 28l

CRÈME DE LA CRÈME À LA EDGAR
Møntergade 10
DK-1116 Copenhagen K
Denmark
+45 33 36 18 18
www.cremedelacremealaedgar.dk
Page 155a both

DANIEL JASIAK
www.danieljasiak.com
Page 56l

DANIELA MICOL WAJSKOL
Interior Designer
Via Vincenzo Monti 42
20123 Milano
danielaw@tiscalinet.it
Page 43r

DEB WATERMAN JOHNS
Get Dressed Wardrobe and
Home & Fifi
1633 29th Street NW
Washington DC 20007
+1 202 625 6425
deb@dogbunny.com
Pages 5ac, 152, 154

EMILY CHALMERS
Author & stylist
Caravan
3 Redchurch Street
Shoreditch
London E2 7DJ
+44 (0)20 7033 3532
www.caravanstyle.com
emily@emilychalmers.com
Pages 136-137

FIL DE FER
Store Kongensgade 83 A
1264 Copenhagen K
Denmark
+45 33 32 32 46
www.fildefer.dk
fildefer@fildefer.dk
Page 10b

FIONA & ALEX COX
www.coxandcox.co.uk
Page 145b

FLINT COLLECTION
49 High Street
Lewes
East Sussex BN7 2DD
www.flintcollection.com
sales@flintcollection.com
Page 55r

GALERIE MIKAEL ANDERSEN
Bredgade 63
DK-1260 Copenhagen
Denmark
+45 33 33 05 12
 www.gma.dk
Page 144

GÉRARD AND DANIÈLLE LABRE
2 Boulevard Alliés
30700 Uzès
France
+33 (0)6 20 69 70 32
glabre@orange.fr
Page 134 both

GRETHE MEYER
Designer and architect MAA
Royal Copenhagen
www.royalcopenhagen.com
Pages 16l, 20al, 63

GUY HILLS
Photographer
Dashing Tweeds
+44 (0)20 7916 2610
www.dashingtweeds.co.uk
guy@dashingtweeds.co.uk
Page 99

HAIFA HAMMAMI
Architect
+44 (0)7730 307612
Pages 76-77

HELEN ELLERY
I Love Home
Interiors and Stylist
helen@helenellery.com
helene@i-love-home.co.uk
Page 2

HEMMINGWAY DESIGN
15 Wembley Park Drive
Wembley HA9 8HD
+44 (0)20 8903 1074
www.hemingwaydesign.co.uk
Page 112

HOGARTH ARCHITECTS LTD
+44 (0)20 7381 3409
www.hogartharchitects.co.uk
info@hogartharchitects.co.uk
Pages 20bl, 44l

HOPE & GREENWOOD
Purveyors of Splendid
Confectionery
www.hopeandgreenwood.co.uk
Page 60

INA CRYSTALS LTD
24 Rochester Square
London NW1 9SA
+44 (0)20 7284 2112
www.liberty.co.uk
Page 141r

INDENFOR & UDENFOR ANTIK
Toldbodgade 65 B
1253 Copenhagen K
Denmark
+45 22 34 94 53
www.indenfor.com
Pages 74br, 91

INGEGERD RAMAN
Bergsgafan 53
SE-11231 Stockholm
Sweden
+46 8 6502824
Ingegerd.raman@orrefors.se
Page 102

JACQUES AZAGURY
50 Knightsbridge
London SW1X 7JN
+ 44 (0)20 7245 1216
 www.jacquesazagury.com
Page 105b both

JAMB
107A Pimlico Road
London SW1W 8PH
+44 (0)20 7730 2122
www.jamblimited.com
Page 115

JAMES SLADE
Slade Architecture
150 Broadway, No. 807
New York, NY 10038
+1 212 677 6380
www.sladearch.com
info@sladearch.com
Page 13r

JANE CUMBERBATCH
www.purestyleonline.com
Page 68

JESTICO + WHILES
www.jesticowhiles.com
Page 71

JOHN NICOLSON
House available to hire as
a location at:
johnnynicolson@aol.com
Pages 8–9, 92

JOHN PEARSE
Tailor
6 Meard Street
W1F OEG
+44 (0)20 7434 0738
www.johnpearse.co.uk
jp@johnpearse .co.uk
Page 121l

JON PELLICORO
jpellicoro@earthlink.net
Page 158

JONATHAN CLARK ARCHITECTS
3rd Floor 34–35 Great Sutton
Street
London EC1V 0DX
+44 (0)20 7608 1111
jonathan@jonathanclark.co.uk
www.jonathanclark.co.uk
Page 125l

JOSEPHINE MACRANDER
Interior Decorator
+31 6 43053062
Pages 4a, 50

JULIAN STAIR
Studio
52A Hindmans Raod
London SE22 9NG
+44 (0)20 8693 4877
www.julianstair.com
studio@julianstair.com
Page 127r

JUNE & DAVID ROSKILDE
Stone Print Lithograph
and Musician and Producer
june@rehak.dk
Page 106r

KATE FORMAN
www.kateforman.co.uk
Page 39r

KATRIN ARENS
www.katrinarens.it
info@katrinarens.it
Pages 22–23 main

KEN FOREMAN
www.kenforemandesign.com
Page 150

KJAERHOLM'S
Rungstedvej 86
DK-2960 Rungsted Kyst
Denmark
+45 45 76 56 56
www.kjaerholms.dk
info@kjaerholms.dk
Pages 51, 113 both

KURT BRENDENBECK
www.kurtbredenbeck.com
Page 81

LENA PROUDLOCK
www.lenaproudlock.com
Pages 142–143

LISA JACKSON LTD
+1 212 593 0117
lcjpeace@aol.com
Page 159

LISETTE PLEASANCE
Boonshill Farm B&B
Near Rye
East Sussex
www.boonshillfarm.co.uk
Page 48

MALCOLM GLIKSTEN
Relic Antiques
127 Pancras Road
+44 (0)7831 785059
malcolm.gliksten@bluyonder.
  co.uk
Page 122a

**MACK SCOGIN MERRILL ELAM
ARCHITECTS**
www.msmearch.com
Page 145a

MARIE-HÉLÈNE DE TAILLAC
www.mariehelenedetaillac.com
Page 42r

MARK SMITH
Smithcreative
15 St George's Road
London W4 1AU
 +44 (0)20 8747 3909
office@smithcreative.net
Pages 52–53

MATALI CRASSET PRODUCTIONS
26 rue du Buisson Saint Louis
75010 Paris
France
+33 1 42 40 99 89
www.matalicrasset.com
matali.crasset@wanadoo.fr
Pages 74bl, 160 both

MELIN TREGWYNT
Castlemorris
Haverfordwest
Pembrokeshire
SA62 5UX
+44 (0)1348 891 644
www.melintregwynt.co.uk
info@melintregwynt.co.uk
Page 31a

MIBO
+44 (0)870011 9620
www.mibo.co.uk
info@mibo.co.uk
Page 109r

**MICHAEL NEUMANN
ARCHITECTURE**
11 East 88th Street
New York, NY 10128
+1 212 828 0407
www.mnarch.com
Page 82

MICHAELIS BOYD ASSOCIATES
Alex Michaelis & Tim Boyd
9B Ladbroke Grove
London W11 3BD
+44 (0)20 7221 1237
www.michaelisboyd.com
info@michaelisboyd.com
Pages 156-157

MMM ARCHITECTS
The Banking Hall
26 Maida Vale
London W9 1RS
+44 (0)20 7286 9499
post@mmmarchitects.com
www.mmmarchitects.com
Pages 84, 85

**MULLMAN SEIDMAN
ARCHITECTS**
137 Varick Street
New York, NY 10013
+1 212 431 0770
www.mullmanseidman.com
Pages 12, 75al, 104

NEISHA CROSLAND
www.neishacrosland.com
Pages 72-73

NICO RENSCH
ARCHITEAM
Campfield House
Powdermill Lane
Battle
East Sussex TN33 0SY
+44 (0)1424 775211
www.architeam.co.uk
nr@architeam.co.uk
Page 163l

**NICOLAS HUG & PHILIPPE
MENAGER**
'Immobilier de Collection'
31 rue de Tournon
75006 Paris
+33 1 53 10 22 60
Pages 75br, 108

NINA HARTMANN
www.vintagebynina.com
Page 54

PHILIPPE GUILMIN
philippe.guilmin@skynet.be
Pages 132-133

PINCH
by appointment
Unit 1W
Clapham North Art Centre
26-32 Voltaire Road
London SW4 6DH
+44 (0) 20 7622 5075
www.pinchdesign.com
Pages 21bl, 27r, 35

PORADA ARREDI S.R.L.
I-22060 Cabiate (Como)
Via P. Buozzi, 2 – Località Porada
+39 031 766215
www.porada.it
Page 18

RACHEL VAN DER BRUG
Interior Design Consultant
Ineke Schierenberg & Rachel van
der Brug VOF
Lange Leidsedwarsstraat 140
1017 NN Amsterdam
+31 (0)20 6390881
www.inekeschierenberg.nl
Pages 88, 89

REINEKE GROTERS
Stylist/artist
reineke.groters@zonnet.nl
Page 149

RETROUVIUS
Architectural reclaimation
and design
2A Ravensworth Road
London NW10 5NR
+44 (0)20 8960 6060
www.retrouvious.com
mail@retrouvius.com
Page 99

RODDY&GINGER
www.roddyandginger.co.uk
virginia@roddyandginger.co.uk
Page 126

**ROELINE FABER INTERIOR
STYLING & DESIGN**
Tweede Molenweg 22
1261 HC Blaricum
The Netherlands
+31 35 6668411
faber.styling@wxs.nl
Page 97

ROSE UNIACKE INTERIORS
8 Holbein Place
London SW1W 8NL
+44 (0)20 7730 7050
www.roseuniacke.com
Pages 74al, 153, 163r

SANDY DAVIDSON DESIGN
www.sandydavidsondesign.com
Pages 78-79

SHAMIR SHAH
www.shamirshahdesign.com
Page 83

SIGMAR
263 Kings Road
London SW3 5EL
+44 (0)20 7751 5802
www.sigmarlondon.com
Page 114 both

STELTON A/S
+45 39 62 30 55
stelton@stelton.dk
www.stelton.com
Pages 20br, 28–29 main

STENHUSET ANTIKHANDEL
Antiques, Interior Design, Lifestlye
Café, B&B
Bögerup 206 A
241 96 Stockamöllan,
Sweden
+ 46 (0)70 965 95 65
www.stenhusetantikhandel.com
Page 58

STEPHEN PARDY
Weston-Pardy Design Consultancy
+44 (0)20 7587 0221
weston.pardy@mac.com
Pages 21br, 57

STEVEN LEARNER STUDIO
307 7th Avenue, Room 2201
New York, NY 10001
www.stevenlearnerstudio.com/
  index.htm
mstevens@stevenlearnerstudio.
  com
Pages 110–111

STEVEN SHAILER
+1 917 518 8001
Page 44ar

STUDIO ARCHITETTURA BENAIM
Via Giotto, 37
50121 Florence
Italy
+39 055 6632 84
benaim@tin.it
Page 120

TAPET CAFÉ
www.tapet-café.dk
Page 56r

TERESA GINORI
Teresa.ginori@aliceposta.it
Pages 100–101

**THE CHILDREN'S COTTAGE
COMPANY** &
SANCTUARY GARDEN OFFICES
www.play-houses.com
www.sanctuarygardenoffices.com
+44 (0)1363 772061
Page 119

THE CROSS &
CROSS THE ROAD
+44 (0)20 7727 6760
Page 4bc

THE MARSTON HOUSE
Main Street at Middle Street
PO Box 517
Wiscasset
Maine 04578
www.marstonhouse.com
Page 62

**THE NEW ENGLAND SHUTTER
COMPANY**
16 Jaggard Way
London SW12 8UB
+44 (0)20 8675 1099
www.tnesc.co.uk
Page 155b

THE SWEDISH CHAIR
+44 (0)20 8657 8560
www.theswedishchair.com
lena@theswedishchair.com
Page 31b

TORE LINDHOLM
tore.lindholm@nchr.uio.no
&
Lund & Hagem Arkitektur AS
www.lundhagem.no
Page 10a

TSÉ &TSÉ ASSOCIEÉS
Catherine Lévy & Sigolène Prébois
www.tse-tse.com
Page 124

TYLER LONDON LTD
www.tylerlondon.com
Page 86

VILLA L'AGACHON
www.villalagachon.com
Page 70

**VIVIEN LAWRENCE INTERIOR
DESIGN**
Interior designer of private
homes-any project from start
to finish, small or large.
London
+44 (0)20 8209 0058/0562
interiordesign@vivienlawrence.
  co.uk
Pages 4b, 122b

VOON WONG
www.vwbs.co.uk
Page 49ar

WEBB ARCHITECTS
www.webb-architects.co.uk
Page 49br

WILLIAM HEFNER
www.williamhefner.com
Pages 78–79

WILLIAM SMALLEY
+44 (0)7753 686711
william@williamsmalley.com
Pages 116–117

WILLIAM W. STUBBS, IIDA
www.wwstubbs.com
Page 86

WIM DEPUYDT
+ 32 495, 777 217
depuydt.architect@pandora.be
Pages 3, 164–165

YANCEY RICHARDSON GALLERY
535 West 22nd Street
New York, NY 10011
www.yanceyrichardson.com
Pages 110–111

PICTURE CREDITS

KEY: *ph*= photographer, **a**=above, **b**=below, **r**=right, **l**=left, **c**=centre.

Endpapers *ph* Polly Wreford/styled by Atlanta Bartlett; **page 1** *ph* Andrew Wood/the home of Andy Marcus & Ron Diliberto in Palm Springs, CA; **2** *ph* Jan Baldwin/designer Helen Ellery's home in London, painting by Robert Clarke; **3** *ph* Winfried Heinze/Val, Wim, Kamilla, Juliette & Joseph's home in Ghent, designed and built by Wim Depuydt, architect; **4a** *ph* Debi Treloar/Wim & Josephine's apartment in Amsterdam; **4ac** *ph* Henry Bourne; **4bc** *ph* Debi Treloar/the London home of Sam Robinson, co-owner of 'The Cross' and 'Cross the Road'; **4b** *ph* Christopher Drake/Vivien Lawrence an interior designer in London (020 8209 0562); **4–5** *ph* Lisa Cohen; **5a** *ph* Debi Treloar/Mark & Sally Bailey's home in Herefordshire; **5ac** *ph* Winfried Heinze/the home of Ben Johns and Deb Waterman Johns; **5bc** *ph* Debi Treloar/Clare & David Mannix-Andrews' house, Hove, East Sussex; **5b** *ph* Polly Wreford/styled by Atlanta Bartlett; **6–7** *ph* Winfried Heinze/the Éclair-Powell home in London; **8–9** *ph* Chris Everard/John Nicolson's house in Spitalfields, London; **10a** *ph* Paul Ryan/summer house at Hvasser, of Astir Eidsbo and Tore Lindholm; **10b** *ph* Winfried Heinze/the apartment of Lars Kristensen owner of Fil de Fer, Copenhagen; **11** *ph* Chris Everard/Ruth Artmonsky's loft in Covent Garden; **12** *ph* Winfried Heinze/Dr Alex Sherman and Ms Ivy Baer Sherman's residence in New York City; Mullman Seidman Architects; **13l** *ph* Winfried Heinze/Isabel & Ricardo Ernst's family home; **13r** *ph* Winfried Heinze/ Glasserman/Gilsanz Residence; architect: James Slade at Cho Slade Architecture, www.sladearch.com; **14** © Case Furniture Ltd – Covet desk by Shin Azumi; **15** *ph* Andrew Wood; **16l** *ph* Andrew Wood/architect Grethe Meyer's house, Hørsholm, Denmark, built by architects Moldenhawer, Hammer and Frederiksen, 1963; **16r** *ph* Debi Treloar/Clare & David Mannix-Andrews' house, Hove, East Sussex; **17** *ph* Chris Everard; **18** © Porada/Pablo writing-desk designed by M.Walraven, Porada; **19 both** *ph* Chris Everard/fashion designer Carla Saibene's home in Milan; **20al** *ph* Andrew Wood/architect Grethe Meyer's house, Hørsholm, Denmark, built by architects Moldenhawer, Hammer and Frederiksen, 1963; **20ar** *ph* Andrew Wood; **20bl** *ph* Dan Duchars/ Ian Hogarth of Hogarth Architects' home office in London; **20br** *ph* Andrew Wood/Peter Holmblad's apartment in Klampenborg, Denmark, designed by architect Arne Jacobsen in 1958; **21al** *ph* Polly Wreford/Foster House at Beach Studios styled by Atlanta Bartlett; **21ar** *ph* Andrew Wood/Ian Bartlett & Christine Walsh, London; **21bl** © Pinch: Pontus desk designed by Russell Pinch, *ph* James Merrell **21br** *ph* Christopher Drake/designer Stephen Pardy's Georgian house in London; **22–23** *ph* Debi Treloar/ design: Cecilia Proserpio, furniture: Katrin Arens; **23** *ph* Debi Treloar/Marcus Hewitt and Susan Hopper's home in Litchfield County, Connecticut; **24** *ph* Polly Wreford/Ann Shore, Story; **25** *ph* Tom Leighton/artist Yuri Kuper; **26** *ph* Mark Scott; **27l** *ph* Polly Wreford; **27r** © Pinch: Yves writing desk designed by Russell Pinch, *ph* James Merrell; **28l** *ph* Chris Everard/ Pemper and Rabiner home in New York, designed by David Khouri of Comma; **28–29 main** *ph* Andrew Wood/Peter Holmblad's apartment in Klampenborg, Denmark, designed by architect Arne Jacobsen in 1958; **30** *ph* Chris Tubbs/Annabel Grey's Norfolk Cottage; **31a** *ph* Claire Richardson/ Eifion & Amanda Griffiths of Melin Tregwynts's house in Wales; **31b** *ph* Debi Treloar/the Swedish Chair – Lena Renkel Eriksson; **32** *ph* Polly Wreford/an apartment in New York designed by Belmont Freeman Architects; **33** *ph* Polly Wreford/styled by Atlanta Bartlett; **34 both** © Case Furniture Ltd – Covet desk by Shin Azumi; **35** © Pinch: Pontus desk designed by Russell Pinch, *ph* James Merrell; **36 & 37** *ph* Debi Treloar/Mark & Sally Bailey's home in Herefordshire; **38–39 main** *ph* Andrew Wood; **39r** *ph* Lisa Cohen/Kate Forman's home; **40 & 41** *ph* Debi Treloar/Catherine Chermayeff & Jonathan David's family home in New York, designed by Asfour Guzy Architects; **42l** *ph* Debi Treloar/ Mark & Sally Bailey's home in Herefordshire; **42r** *ph* Polly Wreford/Marie-Hélène de Taillac's pied-à-terre in Paris; **43l** *ph* Debi Treloar/ the Philadelphia home of Glen Senk & Keith Johnson of Anthropologie; **43r** *ph* Christopher Drake/an apartment in Milan designed by Daniela Micol Wajskol, Interior Designer; **44l** *ph* Dan Duchars/Ian Hogarth of Hogarth Architects' home office in

London; **44ar** *ph* Debi Treloar/ designer Steven Shailer's apartment in New York City; **44br** *ph* Polly Wreford/Clare Nash, London; **45** *ph* Andrew Wood; **46–47** *ph* Andrew Wood/Ian Bartlett & Christine Walsh, London; **48** *ph* Polly Wreford/designer Lisette Pleasance and Mick Shaw's home and B&B; **49al** *ph* Debi Treloar/Cristine Tholstrup Hermansen and Helge Drenck's house in Copenhagen; **49ar** *ph* Jan Baldwin/the Campbell family's apartment in London, architecture by Voon Wong Architects; **49br** *ph* Polly Wreford/a family home in west London by Webb Architects and Cave Interiors; **50** *ph* Debi Treloar/Wim & Josephine's apartment in Amsterdam; **51** *ph* Andrew Wood/the Kjaerholms' family home in Rungsted, Denmark; **52–53** *ph* Dan Duhars/designer Mark Smith's home in London; **54** *ph* Lisa Cohen/ the designer Nina Hartmann's home in Sweden, www.vintagebynina.com; **55l** *ph* Polly Wreford/ Foster House at Beach Studios styled by Atlanta Bartlett; **55r** *ph* Polly Wreford/the home in Lewes of Justin & Heidi Francis, owner of Flint www.flintcollection.com; **56l** *ph* Polly Wreford/ Daniel Jasiak's apartment in Paris; **56r** *ph* Lisa Cohen/owner of TAPET-CAFÉ, textile designer Helene Blanche and husband and Jannik Martensen-Larsen; **57** *ph* Christopher Drake/designer Stephen Pardy's Georgian house in London; **58** *ph* Polly Wreford/ Stenhuset Antikhandel shop, café and B&B in Stockamollan, Sweden; **59** *ph* Jan Baldwin/David Davies's house in East Sussex, England; **60** *ph* Debi Treloar/the owners of 'Hope & Greenwood', Miss Hope & Mr Greenwood's home in London; **61** *ph* Polly Wreford/styled by Atlanta Bartlett, New Cross – location to hire through www.beachstudios.co.uk; **62** *ph* Debi Treloar/Sharon & Paul Mrozinski's home in Bonnieux, France, www.marstonhouse.com; **63** *ph* Andrew Wood/architect Grethe Meyer's house, Hørsholm, Denmark, built by architects Moldenhawer, Hammer and Frederiksen, 1963; **64 & 65** *ph* Ray Main/lighting from Babylon Design; **66** *ph* Polly Wreford/Foster House at Beach Studios styled by Atlanta Bartlett; **67** *ph* Polly Wreford; **68** *ph* Lisa Cohen/designed by Jane Cumberbatch, www.purestyleonline.com; **69** *ph* Polly Wreford/ Foster House at Beach Studios styled by Atlanta Bartlett; **70** *ph* Paul Massey; **71** *ph* James Morris/Tom Jestico & Vivien Fowler's house in London, design team Tom Jestico & Vivien Fowler; **72–73** *ph* Christopher Drake/Neisha Crosland; **74al** *ph*

Winfried Heinze/Rose Uniacke's home in London; **74ar** *ph* Debi Treloar/the Philadelphia home of Glen Senk & Keith Johnson of Anthropologie; **74bl** *ph* Winfried Heinze/interior architecture: matali crasset; **74br** *ph* Polly Wreford/Indenfor & Udenfor in Copenhagen (home and shop near the royal castle); **75al** *ph* Chris Everard/an apartment in New York, designed by Mullman Seidman Architects; **75ar** *ph* Andrew Wood/a house in Stockholm, Sweden; **75bl** *ph* Polly Wreford/the home in Provençe of Carolyn Oswald; **75br** *ph* Andrew Wood/the Paris apartment of Nicolas Hug; **76–77** *ph* Dan Duhars/architect Haifa Hammami's home in London; **78–79 all** *ph* James Morris/Joan Barnett's house in West Hollywood, designed by William R. Hefner AIA, interior design by Sandy Davidson Design; **80** *ph* Andrew Wood/the home of Sean and Tricia Brunson in Orlando; **81** *ph* Andrew Wood/Kurt Bredenbeck's apartment at the Barbican, London; **82** *ph* Jan Baldwin/Alfredo Paredes and Brad Goldfarb's loft in Tribeca, New York designed by Michael Neumann Architecture; **83** *ph* Chris Everard/a New York apartment designed by Shamir Shah; **84–85** *ph* Polly Wreford/Ingrid and Avinash Persaud's home in London; **86** *ph* Christopher Drake/a house in London architectural design and procurement by Tyler London Ltd, interior design by William W. Stubbs, IIDA; **87** *ph* Debi Treloar; **88 & 89** *ph* Claire Richardson/ interior design consultant Rachel van der Brug's home in Amsterdam; **90** *ph* Polly Wreford/Charlotte-Anne Fidler's home in London; **91** *ph* Polly Wreford/ Indenfor & Udenfor in Copenhagen (home and shop near the royal castle); **92** *ph* Chris Everard/John Nicolson's house in Spitalfields, London; **93** *ph* Debi Treloar/Robert Elms and Christina Wilson's family home in London; **94–95** *ph* Andrew Wood/a house in Stockholm, Sweden; **96** *ph* Polly Wreford/Foster House at Beach Studios styled by Atlanta Bartlett; **97** *ph* Debi Treloar/Roeline Faber, interior designer; **98** *ph* Jan Baldwin/Alison Hill & John Taylor's home in Greenwich; **99** *ph* Chris Everard/ photographer Guy Hills' house in London designed by Joanna Rippon & Maria Speake of Retrouvius; **100–101** *ph* Chris Tubbs/Teresa Ginori's home near Varese, parchment shade by architect Roberto Gerosa; **102** *ph* Paul Ryan/the home of Ingegerd Raman and Claes Söderquist's home in Sweden; **103** *ph* Tom Leighton/ Netty Nauta; **104** *ph* Chris Everard/an apartment in New York, designed by Mullman Seidman Architects;

105a *ph* Andrew Wood/Jo Shane, John Cooper and family, apartment in New York; 105b both *ph* Winfried Heinze/the apartment of Jacques Azagury in London; 106l *ph* Andrew Wood; 106r *ph* Polly Wreford/the home in Copenhagen of June and David; 107 *ph* Polly Wreford/Foster House at Beach Studios styled by Atlanta Bartlett; 108 *ph* Andrew Wood/the Paris apartment of Nicolas Hug; 109l *ph* Debi Treloar/Hélène & Konrad Adamczewski, Lewes; 109r *ph* Debi Treloar/Madeleine Rogers of Mibo; 110–111 *ph* Winfried Heinze/the apartment of Yancey and Mark Richardson in New York, architecture and interior design by Steven Learner Studio paintings by Vic Muniz and Adam Fuss, three nudes on desk by Alvin Booth; 112 *ph* Winfried Heinze/Wayne & Gerardine Hemingway of Hemingway Design's home in Sussex; 113 both *ph* Andrew Wood/ the Kjaerholms' family home in Rungsted, Denmark; 114 both *ph* Winfried Heinze/the Notting Hill flat of Ebba Thott from "Sigmar" in London; 115 *ph* Christopher Drake/antique dealer and co-owner of Jamb Ltd /Antique Chimneypieces; 116–117 *ph* Jan Baldwin/ architect William Smalley's London flat; 118 *ph* Andrew Wood/an original Florida home restored by Andrew Weaving of Century, www.centuryd.com; 119 *ph* Chris Tubbs; 120 *ph* Chris Tubbs/Podere Sala, Lori De Mori's home in Tuscany restored by architect André Benaim; 121l *ph* Winfried Heinze/Florence & John Pearse's apartment in London; 121r *ph* Chris Tubbs/Toia Saibene & Giuliana Magnifico's home in Lucignano, Tuscany; 122a *ph* Claire Richardson/Malcolm Gliksten's home in France; 122b *ph* Christopher Drake/Vivien Lawrence an interior designer in London (020 8209 0562); 123 *ph* James Merrell; 124 *ph* Debi Treloar/Sigolène Prébois of Tsé &Tsé associeés home in Paris; 125l *ph* Chris Everard/architect Jonathan Clark's home in London; 125r *ph* Polly Wreford/the family home of Alison Smith in Brighton; 126 *ph* Polly Wreford/the South London home of designer Virginia Armstrong of roddy&ginger; 127l *ph* Lisa Cohen/Clara Baillie's house on the Isle of Wight; 127r *ph* Debi Treloar/the home and studio of Julian Stair in London; 128–131 *ph* Tom Leighton/ artist Yuri Kuper; 132–133 *ph* Debi Treloar/the guesthouse of the interior designer & artist Philippe Guilmin, Brussels; 134 both Claire Richardson/Gérard and Danièlle Labre's home near Uzès in France; 135 *ph* Debi Treloar/the Philadelphia home of Glen Senk & Keith Johnson of Anthropologie; 136–137 *ph* Debi Treloar/author, stylist and 'Caravan' (shop) owner Emily Chalmers and director Chris Richmond's former home in London; 138 *ph* Polly Wreford/the home in Provençe of Carolyn Oswald; 139 *ph* Debi Treloar/Mark & Sally Bailey's home in Herefordshire; 140 *ph* Polly Wreford/the home in Provençe of Carolyn Oswald; 141l *ph* Lisa Cohen/Clara Baillie's house on the Isle of Wight; 141r *ph* Polly Wreford/the family home of Azzi & Dan Glasser in North London; 142–143 *ph* Polly Wreford/Lena Proudlock; 144 *ph* Andrew Wood/gallery owner Mikael Andersen's studio house in Denmark, designed by Henning Larsen; 145a *ph* James Morris/ Nomentana Residence in Maine designed by Mack Scogin Merrill Elam Architects; 145b *ph* Polly Wreford/the family home of Fiona and Alex Cox of www.coxandcox.co.uk; 146 *ph* Debi Treloar/private house in Amsterdam owner, Ank de la Plume; 147 *ph* Debi Treloar/the home of Netty Nauta in Amsterdam; 148 *ph* Polly Wreford/Foster House at Beach Studios styled by Atlanta Bartlett; 149 *ph* Debi Treloar/the home in Amsterdam of the stylist/artist Reineke Groters; 150 *ph* Polly Wreford/ Kathy Moskal's apartment in New York designed by Ken Foreman; 151 *ph* Caroline Arber/designed and styled by Jane Cassini and Ann Brownfield; 152 *ph* Winfried Heinze/the home of Ben Johns and Deb Waterman Johns; 153 *ph* Winfried Heinze/Rose Uniacke's home in London; 154 *ph* Debi Treloar/the home of Ben Johns and Deb Waterman Johns; 155a both *ph* Debi Treloar/owner of Crème de la Crème à la Edgar, Helle Høgsbro Krag's home in Copenhagen; 155b *ph* Winfried Heinze/Sophie Eadie's home in London; 156–157 *ph* Winfried Heinze/the O'Connor Bandeen family home in London; 158 *ph* Winfried Heinze/Jon Pellicoro artist & designer; 159 *ph* Winfried Heinze/interior designer Lisa Jackson's home in New York; 160 both *ph* Winfried Heinze/ interior architecture: matali crasset; 161 *ph* Winfried Heinze/Freddie Hair's room in London; 162 *ph* Winfried Heinze/the Fried family home in London; 163l *ph* Winfried Heinze/architect and interiors: Nico Rensch, Architeam; 163r *ph* Winfried Heinze/Rose Uniacke's home in London; 164–165 *ph* Winfried Heinze/Val, Wim, Kamilla, Juliette and Joseph's home in Ghent, designed and built by Wim Depuydt, architect.

ACKNOWLEDGMENTS

Writing this book – in the comfort of my own brand new, fantastically wonderful, study – made me appreciate anew the care and attention to detail that a good publishing team lavishes on every book they produce. I was lucky enough to have Alison Starling, Rebecca Woods, Leslie Harrington and Paul Tilby, and of course the indefatigable Emily Westlake.

Thank you all so much.

ABOUT THE AUTHOR

Caroline Clifton-Mogg is an acclaimed journalist and author who writes about interior design and gardens, among other subjects. She contributes to various magazines including *House & Garden*. Her books include *Tuscan Escapes*, *French Country Living*, *The Comforts of Home* and *All in the Detail* (all published by Ryland Peters & Small).

SUPER SATIN

JAMES WHITE   2010

MATCHSTICK   2013

BLACKENED   2011

HAY